CHARLES F. STANLEY BIBLE STUDY SERIES

MINISTERING THROUGH SPIRITUAL GIFTS

USE YOUR STRENGTHS TO SERVE OTHERS

CHARLES F. STANLEY

THOMAS NELSON
Since 1798

MINISTERING THROUGH SPIRITUAL GIFTS
CHARLES F. STANLEY BIBLE STUDY SERIES

Copyright © 2010, 2020 by Charles F. Stanley.

All rights reserved. No portion of this book may be reproduced, stored in a retrieval system, or transmitted in any form or by any means—electronic, mechanical, photocopy, recording, scanning, or other—except for brief quotations in critical reviews or articles, without the prior written permission of the publisher.

Published in Nashville, Tennessee, by Thomas Nelson. Thomas Nelson is a registered trademark of HarperCollins Christian Publishing, Inc.

All Scripture quotations are taken from the New King James Version.® Copyright © 1982 by Thomas Nelson. Used by permission. All rights reserved worldwide.

Thomas Nelson titles may be purchased in bulk for educational, business, fundraising, or sales promotional use. For information, e-mail SpecialMarkets@ThomasNelson.com.

ISBN 978-0-310-10566-4 (softcover)
ISBN 978-0-310-10567-1 (ebook)

First Printing August 2020 / Printed in the United States of America

HB 04.25.2024

CONTENTS

THE HOPE OF GREATER STRENGTH

A number of books are available today to help you understand your talents and abilities and learn how to use them to achieve success. This book is unlike them in two ways. First, it is intended as a personal Bible study, not as a standalone book. Second, it is intended to help you discover the spiritual gifts that God has given you so you can use them for the body of Christ as a whole—not just your own personal success. The intent for using any spiritual gift is not personal gain but the building up of others within the church.

Note these gifts are *spiritual* in nature, so they are not going to be understood by anyone who does not have a relationship with Christ. The Holy Spirit is the One who reveals the spiritual gifts and their use—and those who have not accepted Christ as their Savior do not yet have the Holy Spirit residing within them. Therefore, this study should only be undertaken by those who are followers of Christ and who desire both to know and to use their gifts effectively.

In this study, we will use the terms *motivational gifts* and *ministry gifts* interchangeably. These are the spiritual gifts that *motivate* you to minister to others. They are *ministry* gifts in that they are always intended to build up others in the body of Christ.

This book can be used by you alone or by several people in a small-group study. At various times, you will be asked to relate to the material in one of the following four ways.

First, what new insights have you gained? Make notes about the insights you have. You may want to record them in your Bible or in a separate journal. As you reflect on your new understanding, you are likely to see how God has moved in your life.

Second, have you ever had a similar experience? You approach the Bible from your own unique background . . . your own particular set of understandings about the world that you bring with you when you open God's Word. For this reason, it is important to consider how your experiences are shaping your understanding and allow yourself to be open to the truth that God reveals.

Third, how do you feel about the material? While you should not depend solely on your emotions as a gauge for your faith, it is important for you to be aware of them as you study a passage of Scripture and can freely express them to God. Sometimes, the Holy Spirit will use your emotions to compel you to look at your life in a different or challenging way.

Fourth, in what way do you feel challenged to respond or to act? God's Word may inspire you or challenge you to take a particular action. Take this challenge seriously and find ways to move into it. If God reveals a particular need that He wants you to address, take that as His "marching orders." God will empower you to do something with the challenge that He has just given you.

Start your Bible study sessions in prayer. Ask God to give you spiritual eyes to see and spiritual ears to hear. As you conclude your study, ask the Lord to seal what you have learned so you will not forget it. Ask Him to help you grow into the fullness of the nature and character of Christ Jesus.

I encourage you to keep the Bible at the center of your study. A genuine Bible study stays focused on God's Word and promotes a growing faith and a closer walk with the Holy Spirit in each person who participates.

GOD'S SPECIAL GIFT TO YOU

IN THIS LESSON

Learning: What exactly are motivational gifts?

Growing: Where do motivational gifts come from?

Do you know your innate spiritual gift? Have you identified the most important gift that God has given to you for the purposes of ministry in His name? Every Christian has been given a spiritual gift from God—a gift designed to be used as part of the body of Christ and for the purpose of assisting others. All believers receive these gifts the moment they accept Jesus Christ as their personal Savior. These gifts are intended to be the main avenue through which a person ministers to others within the church as a whole.

I refer to these gifts as "motivational gifts," for they are intended to motivate you toward service. They are gifts that compel and inspire you to act in specific ways. They are the particular bent that you have to serve God's people and others whom you desire to see become Christians. I believe it is vitally important to your personal spiritual life—as well as to the overall spiritual life of the church—for you to recognize these gifts, to encourage their proper use in the church, and encourage one another as you exercise them.

1. Do you know what your motivational gift is? If so, how are you using it at present?

_____

_____

_____

_____

_____

_____

_____

_____

_____

2. What are some ways that you have sensed God *motivating* you toward service?

_____

_____

_____

_____

_____

_____

_____

_____

_____

_____

Nature of Motivational Gifts

Several things about these motivational gifts are vital for us to acknowledge at the outset of our study. First, *every person has received a motivational gift.* Some people may seem gifted with a number of these types of gifts, but there is going to be one covered in this study that will be dominant in a person's life. The Lord instills that gift in a person at his or her birth, and it becomes fully operative for its God-given purposes when that person is born again.

Second, the motivational gifts are intended to be used in the church for building up God's people. As the apostle Paul wrote, "The manifestation of the Spirit is given to each one for the profit of all" (1 Corinthians 12:7). Each of the motivational gifts may be employed "in the flesh," or employed by the person for his or own personal gain. When this happens, disaster follows. The misuse of the gifts is actually counterproductive to the work the Holy Spirit desires to do in us individually and in the church as a whole. We must thus rely completely on the Holy Spirit to assist us in the use of our motivational gifts.

Third, God has commanded us to use these gifts. Peter wrote, "As each one has received a gift, minister it to one another, as good stewards of the manifold grace of God" (1 Peter 4:10). Paul advised Timothy, "Do not neglect the gift that is in you, which was given to you by prophecy with the laying on of the hands of eldership" (1 Timothy 4:14). The Bible is clear that God has given us the motivational gifts for a purpose. We are not to neglect our responsibility to uncover our gifts and learn how to use them effectively in the church.

Fourth, the motivational gifts reside in the believer. The New Testament identifies certain gifts that reside in the *Holy Spirit.* Such gifts operate "as the Spirit wills" and may be manifested in a believer's life from time to time (see 1 Corinthians 12:8–11 for a list of these types of gifts). However, the motivational gifts are built into our personalities as believers in Christ and are permanent. For instance, we will not manifest the motivational gift of prophecy for six months, and then shift to a motivational gift of service for the next three years, and then shift to another gift. Furthermore, the motivational gifts span the course of our lives. They may manifest in slightly different ways, in different situations, with varying degrees of intensity, but the identity of the gift remains intact and is unchangeable.

Fifth, we each have a responsibility to discover and use our spiritual gifts. The more we learn about our spiritual gifts, the greater the responsibility we have to use them for the benefit of others. The first thing we must recognize is that we have a motivational gift given to us by God. We must then recognize which of the seven gifts have been given to us. This is a major step for many believers who have never considered themselves to be "gifted" by God in any particular way. But let me repeat: *you* have been given a motivational gift by God. *You* bear this as part of your identity. *You* are responsible for identifying your gift, developing it, and using it for the glory of God. The more you use your motivational gift, the more you will grow in it, and the more the Holy Spirit will be able to use you in it.

3. "The manifestation of the Spirit is given to each one for the profit of all" (1 Corinthians 12:7). What does this say about the nature of spiritual gifts?

4. "Do not neglect the gift that is in you, which was given to you by prophecy with the laying on of the hands of the eldership" (1 Timothy 4:14). Why do you think it is important to use the particular gift or gifts that God has provided to you?

....

....

....

....

....

....

....

....

....

No Spectators Allowed

The church was not designed by God to include spectators. Every person within the church—which is the greater body of Christ—is expected to be vibrantly alive and active, each one using his or her motivational gift at all times and in as many situations as possible, and each believer being open to use by the Holy Spirit as He wills in the manifestation of other spiritual gifts.

So many people in the church today are sitting on the sidelines, just watching others take active roles. In fact, it has been estimated that eighty percent of those who attend church regularly watch the other twenty percent do the work. The phenomenon is called the "80/20 Rule." Jesus understood this tendency of people—even those among His followers—to want to sit back and just observe what is happening around them. As we read in the Gospel of Luke, "After these things the Lord appointed seventy others also, and sent them two by two . . . Then He said to them, 'The harvest truly is great, but the laborers are few; therefore pray the Lord of the harvest to send out laborers into His harvest'" (Luke 10:1–2).

In many ways, it is similar to athletes who choose to sit out for all or part of the season. While there may be good reasons for these athletes to make this choice, in the end their decision not to use their particular gifts, talents, and abilities is detrimental to the team. Team sports are dependent on all of the members showing up and doing their particular roles. When one person is missing, it is like a puzzle that is missing a piece. The other players on the team have to stretch and adapt to fill the missing player's role.

When believers in Christ choose not to use their gifts, it is detrimental to themselves, to those in the church who are active, and to the work of the Lord as a whole. It certainly is not God's desire or design. Rather, God desires for all believers to be active in the use of their gifts so they will grow more and more into the fullness of what He intended in their lives from the moment of their creation. He desires for the work within the church to be evenly distributed so that no one reaches the state of overload or burn out. And He desires that the work of the church as a whole will be balanced, vibrant, and effective to reach the lost for Christ.

5. "As each one has received a gift, minister it to one another, as good stewards of the manifold grace of God" (1 Peter 4:10). What does it mean to minister your gifts "to one another"? How is this done? Why is it important?

6. What does Peter mean by "the manifold grace of God"? What does God's grace have to do with your spiritual gifts?

WORK AS GOD GIVES THE ENERGY

I like what the psalmist says about doing the work that God has given us to do: "The righteous shall flourish like a palm tree, He shall grow like a cedar in Lebanon. Those who are planted in the house of the LORD shall flourish in the courts of our God. They shall still bear fruit in old age; they shall be fresh and flourishing, to declare that the LORD is upright; He is my rock, and there is no unrighteousness in Him" (Psalm 92:12–15).

We're to work as long as God gives us the energy. Even in "old age," we can still bear good fruit for Christ. We can be "fresh and flourishing" in our mission. How do we do this? Well, science tells us that if we want to lead a long and healthy life, we have to eat right, exercise every day, and avoid doing things that will be detrimental to our physical state of being. The same is true of our spiritual lives. If we want to flourish and continue to bear good fruit for God, we read His Word, pray, fellowship with other believers in Christ, and avoid doing those things that would be detrimental to our spiritual state of being. In other words, we have to engage in "spiritual exercise" every day . . . which involves operating in our gifts.

My desire for you is that you look at yourself and say, "God, here is who I am today. What do You want to do in my life? Where do You want me to go? I refuse to accept the excuse that I am too old, too weak, or too inexperienced to do what You have called me to do. I refuse to allow fear to hold me back from using the gifts that You have given to me. I know that I have talents, and I have the Holy Spirit in me. So, I'm going to give it my best beginning today. I'm listening for direction. I'm going to trust You. I'm going to obey you."

Today could be a life-changing day. It's a choice you make.

7. "Let us not grow weary while doing good, for in due season we shall reap if we do not lose heart. Therefore, as we have opportunity, let us do good to all, especially to those who are of the household of faith" (Galatians 6:9–10). What are some ways that believers in Christ might get "weary" in doing good for others?

8. What does this passage say will happen if you refuse to give up and persevere in using the talents, gifts, and abilities that God has provided to you?

Do Try This at Home!

Remember that the motivational gifts were never designed to be used *independently* but with *others* to build up the church. The church is not a building or an organization. It is a living spiritual entity—just like the body is a living physical entity—and it is composed of all people who believe in the Lord Jesus Christ as the Son of God and the Savior sent by God to reconcile mankind to Himself. Remember, genuine "church members" are wherever you find believers in Jesus Christ. Sometimes that will be at work, or in the community as a whole.

Your ministry gift is thus to function in *all* settings, not merely when you are serving on a church committee or as a part of a church-sponsored program. Whatever your gift may be, find ways to employ it in love, humility, and peace to those around you and in conjunction with other members of the body of Christ.

You and your spouse are likely to have different ministry gifts. Openly acknowledge your differences and find ways you can work together, building up one another and your family, rather than tearing one another down through criticism or competition. You and your children may very well have different ministry gifts. Again, openly acknowledge your gift and seek ways of employing them in a harmonious way that builds up your family life.

Your ministry gifts are intended to bring glory to God. So always make that your goal. Exercise your gifts as you believe Jesus would manifest them. Do what He would do and say what He would say. Always use your ministry gift with the fullness of the character of the Holy Spirit: "love, joy, peace, longsuffering, kindness, goodness, faithfulness, gentleness, self-control" (Galatians 5:22–23). If you use your gift while manifesting the true character of our Lord, you will be a blessing to others, and you will reap the Lord's rewards and blessings in return.

This study is designed to help you *understand* the spiritual gifts, *identify* your particular gift, and *motivate* you to use that gift. I believe that two things will happen as you understand who you are in Jesus Christ and what your identity is within the body of Christ. First, you are going to be excited about your identity and the ways in which God desires to use you. Second, you are going to be challenged to develop your gift and employ it to the best of your ability. God has many special rewards reserved for those who employ their motivational ministry gifts to the best of their abilities. So don't miss out on them!

9. "I remind you to stir up the gift of God which is in you through the laying on of my hands. For God has not given us a spirit of fear, but of power and of love and of a sound mind" (2 Timothy 1:6–7). What does it mean to "stir up the gift of God which is in you"? How is this done? Why might it need to be stirred up?

10. How can fear interfere with your use of God's gifts? What role is played by "a sound mind" in eradicating such fear? How is it done?

16

TODAY AND TOMORROW

Today: Every Christian is given a motivational gift by the Holy Spirit, intended for use in building up others.

Tomorrow: I will spend time in prayer and reflection this week, asking the Lord to show me what motivational gift He has given me.

CLOSING PRAYER

Father, we thank You and praise You for the amazing gifts that You have given to every one of us. Teach us today the nature of these gifts. Let our minds be open to receive Your instruction and our hearts be open to put those instructions into action. We desire today to be operating the gifts that You have given. We pray that You will reveal these gifts to us and put us into situations where we can use them. We don't want to be "spectators" but active in Your plans.

NOTES AND PRAYER REQUESTS

Use this space to write any key points, questions, or prayer requests from this week's study.

An Overview of the Ministry Gifts

IN THIS LESSON

Learning: What does it mean to be in the "body of Christ"?

Growing: How can I use my spiritual gift within that body?

The apostle Paul first identified the motivational gifts in his letter to the believers in Rome. However, he prefaced his definition of these gifts with an important admonition: "For as we have many members in one body, but all the members do not have the same function, so we, being many, are one body in Christ, and individually members of one another" (Romans 12:4–5).

At the outset of our study, I want you to focus on Paul's statement that "all the members do not have the same function" and yet all are "one body in Christ." We can be different and yet be united! We have different gifts and roles to play within the church, yet there are many things that we share in common. As concerned as Paul was about our individual gifts, he was equally concerned that the church regard itself as a whole and function as a whole.

1. Recall a situation in which diversity and unity were both present. What enabled people to be different yet united together?

_____

_____

_____

_____

_____

_____

_____

2. When have you seen division caused by people with different skills, aptitudes, or goals? What caused the division? How might people have become more unified together?

_____

_____

_____

_____

_____

_____

_____

SEVEN GIFTS GIVEN FOR MINISTRY PURPOSES

It is against this backdrop of a unified body that Paul then identifies seven motivational gifts. He writes, "Having then gifts differing according to the grace that is given to us, let us use them: if prophecy, let us prophesy in proportion to our faith; or ministry, let us use it in our ministering; he who teaches, in teaching; he who exhorts, in exhortation; he who gives, with liberality; he who leads, with diligence; he who shows mercy, with cheerfulness" (Romans 12:6–8).

Note clearly the seven gifts that Paul identifies: (1) prophecy; (2) ministering, which may also be called service; (3) teaching; (4) exhortation; (5) giving; (6) leading, which may also be called administration or organization; and (7) mercy. Paul further states that we each have one of these gifts "according to the grace that is given to us" (verse 6). God is the giver of the gifts, and through the Holy Spirit, He helps us identify, develop, and use our gifts. These are not gifts that we "work up" or choose for ourselves. They are gifts from God to us. We must recognize how we are made, embrace our own gift, and then seek to grow in it.

The following are seven passages found in the New Testament that relate to each of these seven motivational gifts. Some of the verses are in contexts other than spiritual gifts—such as that of eldership or the fruit of the Spirit—but the principles described for each gift will serve as an overview introduction to how that gift should be used. As you read through these passages, recognize that motivational gifts are to be used in all contexts of your life—at home, in one-on-one encounters, and on the job—but *especially* in the church.

- *Prophecy:* "Pursue love, and desire spiritual gifts, but especially that you may prophesy. For he who speaks in a tongue does not speak to men but to God, for no one understands him; however, in the spirit he speaks mysteries. But he who prophesies speaks edification and exhortation and comfort to men (1 Corinthians 14:1–3).

- *Ministering or Serving:* "For you, brethren, have been called to liberty; only do not use liberty as an opportunity for the flesh, but through love serve one another. For all the law is fulfilled in one word, even in this: 'You shall love your neighbor as yourself.' But if you bite and devour one another, beware lest you be consumed by one another!" (Galatians 5:13–15).

- *Teaching:* "I do not write these things to shame you, but as my beloved children I warn you. For though you might have ten thousand instructors in Christ, yet you do not have many fathers. . . . For this reason I have sent Timothy to you, who is my beloved and faithful son in the Lord, who will remind you of my ways in Christ, as I teach everywhere in every church" (1 Corinthians 4:14–15, 17).

- *Exhorting:* "Beware, brethren, lest there be in any of you an evil heart of unbelief in departing from the living God; but exhort one another daily, while it is called 'Today,' lest any of you be hardened through the deceitfulness of sin" (Hebrews 3:12–13).

- *Giving:* "But this I say: He who sows sparingly will also reap sparingly, and he who sows bountifully will also reap bountifully. So let each one give as he purposes in his heart, not grudgingly or of necessity; for God loves a cheerful giver" (2 Corinthians 9:6–7).

- *Leading:* "A bishop then must be blameless . . . one who rules his own house well, having his children in submission with all reverence (for if a man does not know how to rule his own house, how will he take care of the church of God?) . . . Moreover he must have a good testimony among those who are outside, lest he fall into reproach" (1 Timothy 3:2, 4–5, 7).

• *Mercy:* "Therefore, as the elect of God, holy and beloved, put on tender mercies, kindness, humility, meekness, longsuffering; bearing with one another, and forgiving one another, if anyone has a complaint against another; even as Christ forgave you, so you also must do" (Colossians 3:12–13).

3. What themes do you find in all these verses concerning the proper use of spiritual gifts?

....

....

....

....

....

....

....

....

4. "For as the body is one and has many members, but all the members of that one body, being many, are one body, so also is Christ. For by one Spirit we were all baptized into one body" (1 Corinthians 12:12–13). Picture yourself walking. How do different parts of your body participate in that activity? What do your arms do? Your hips? Your eyes?

....

....

....

....

....

....

....

....

5. How is this a metaphor for the proper use of spiritual gifts? How might the seven different gifts listed above work together in some single ministry?

....

....

....

....

....

....

....

....

DISCOVERING YOUR PARTICULAR GIFT

Do not be alarmed if you are not able to identify your own motivational gift at this point. You will have ample opportunity to zero in on your gift in the lessons that follow. For now, just recognize there may be some reasons as to why you don't know your gift.

First, you may have a "cloudy" relationship with God. As previously noted, all believers in Christ have been indwelt by the Holy Spirit and given a ministry gift. However, you won't be able to identify your specific gift (or gifts) if you have not first accepted Jesus as your Savior. If you are unsure about you position in Christ, I encourage you to take action today. Accept Jesus Christ as your Savior. Invite the Holy Spirit to guide you and remind you daily of your reliance on Him. Study God's Word to discover your position in Jesus Christ.

Second, you may not be involved in service to others. Jesus said, "Give, and it will be given to you: good measure, pressed down, shaken together, and running over will be put into your bosom. For with the same measure that you use, it will be measured back to you" (Luke 6:38). Much of what you will discover about yourself—and particularly about your ministry gift—will be learned only as you attempt to help others. It is as you *give* to others and pour out your life that you *receive* it back and begin to understand the things of God.

Third, you may be attempting to imitate another person. Perhaps there is a person in your life whom you admire greatly. Maybe this is even the person who led you to Christ. As long as you are trying to copy the ministry gift of another person, you will not be in a position to recognize and develop your own gift from God. The Lord has called you for a specific purpose and gifted you for that purpose. So your gifts will not always be the same as others receive.

Fourth, you may have failed to recognize the motivation for your actions. Discovering your motivational gift requires a certain degree of introspection and self-examination. You need to understand your motives. Make your prayer in this regard the same as King David once prayed: "Search me, O God, and know my heart; try me, and know my anxieties; and see if there is any wicked way in me, and lead me in the way everlasting" (Psalm 139:23–24).

Fifth, you may be confused about the difference between a ministry and a gift. A *ministry* is a specific act of service to others, such as working with the children's choir or feeding the homeless. A ministry *gift* is the motivation that leads you to engage in a facet of ministry. For example, if you are involved in the children's choir, you may have the gift of *leading*. If so, you are likely to administer and organize the program, and you may be the choirmaster. Or you may have a gift of *service*. If so, you are likely the one who makes sure the choir robes are clean and that refreshments are available after the rehearsals.

Finally, you may have a false understanding of who receives ministry gifts. Some Christians believe that only full-time clergy and staff members in a church are gifted or qualified for ministry. However, as we have seen, the ministry gifts are given to *all* members of the church. Every person has a gift and is commanded to use that gift. Church roles are identified elsewhere in Scripture as apostles, prophets, evangelists, pastors, and teachers. But even within these roles, a person will have a tendency to gravitate toward a particular motivational gift.

6. Which of the above misconceptions have you struggled with the most? Explain.

7. How has such faulty thinking hindered the use of your spiritual gift in the past?

8. What will you do this week to correct those faulty ways of thinking? How will you seek to use your gift in *service* to the Lord?

How the Gifts Work Together

The motivational gifts are designed to work together, complement each other, and be joined together in productive ways to benefit the whole body of Christ. When we develop and exercise our motivational gifts, we bring refinement and balance to the church as a whole. As we do this, we need to keep in mind three key words that were emphasized by Jesus, Paul, and other New Testament writers in regard to how we treat one another and minister to one another.

The first of these is love. We are to treat others with love at all times. Love must be our attitude, the tone of our voice, the purpose for our actions, and the goal that we seek in all relationships. *The second is humility.* We are to treat others with respect, gentleness, and patience. The third is *peace.* We are to create an overall atmosphere of peace and reconciliation within the church. The gifts were never intended to divide God's people, but rather to heal, restore, nurture, unify, and build them up as a strong and vibrant whole.

As Paul wrote, the exercise of our gifts without love and humility results in our coming across as "sounding brass or a clanging cymbal" (1 Corinthians 13:1). These are obnoxious sounds that only interrupt and bring discord. Love, however, builds up and brings peace. Any exercise of our motivational gifts without love brings no benefit to us or others. For our ministry gifts to be effective and to be a blessing, we must choose to love, we must work for peace, and we must remain humble in our relationships with others.

When we use our motivational gifts in godly ways, we experience minimum weariness and maximum effectiveness. We find deep inner satisfaction and contentment. We see the purpose for our lives being fulfilled and have a great sense of meaningfulness.

9. "This is My commandment, that you love one another as I have loved you. Greater love has no one than this, than to lay down one's life for his friends" (John 15:12–13). What does it mean, in practical terms, to love others as Jesus loves you?

10. How might exercising your spiritual gift involve laying down your life for others (either literally or figuratively)?

TODAY AND TOMORROW

Today: The Lord has given me a ministry gift,
and I must learn to use it to bring strength and
health to the body of Christ.

Tomorrow: I will spend time this week asking the Lord
to show me how to use my gift in service to Him.

CLOSING PRAYER

Father, we thank You for not just saving us and then leaving us here on earth to manage the best we can. You did something so amazing when You sent Jesus to forgive us of our sins and You sent the Holy Spirt to dwell within us and empower us. We know that He enables us to do every single thing that You have called us to do. We continue to pray that we will come to understand our motivational gift, know clearly the avenue by which we should express that gift, and look with anticipation to the results You will bring as we obey You.

NOTES AND
PRAYER REQUESTS

Use this space to write any key points, questions, or prayer requests from this week's study.

THE GIFT OF PROPHECY

IN THIS LESSON

Learning: Does a prophet foretell future events?

Growing: What function does a prophet
have in the church today?

Do you find that you can't remain quiet or sit still when you are hearing a lie or are in the presence of evil? Do you have a clear-cut understanding of what God considers to be right and wrong? If so, you may have been given the gift of prophecy.

Prophets are those who speak the truth. Many people understand *prophecy* to be "foretelling the future." For example, in the book of 1 Kings, we read how the prophet Elijah said to King Ahab, "As the Lord God of Israel lives, before whom I stand, there shall not be dew nor rain these years, except at my word" (17:1). These words came to pass, and for three long years there was a drought in Israel. Later, in the book of Acts, we read how the prophet Agabus foretold the apostle Paul's arrest in Jerusalem. Luke tells us, "He took Paul's belt, bound his own hands and feet, and said, 'Thus says the Holy Spirit, "So shall the Jews at Jerusalem bind the man who owns this belt, and deliver him into the hands of the Gentiles""'" (Acts 21:11).

However, the more general meaning for *prophecy* in the Bible is "forth-telling," which means to proclaim the principles of God that are true now and forever. For example, in the Gospel of Mark, we read how John the Baptist was a prophet who called the people to repentance. "John came baptizing in the wilderness and preaching a baptism of repentance for the remission of sins. . . . And he preached, saying, 'There comes One after me who is mightier than I, whose sandal strap I am not worthy to stoop down and loose. I indeed baptized you with water, but He will baptize you with the Holy Spirit'" (Mark 1:4, 7–8).

Regardless of whether the prophet engages in foretelling or forth-telling, genuine prophets of God *must* speak the truth. They cannot remain quiet in the face of a lie, or any form of deceit, or in the face of an error against God's Word. Prophets are often those who see things in terms or black-and-white or right-and-wrong. They are motivated to set things right and get the church back on the right track. They speak boldly in the presence of injustice.

1. What comes to mind when you think of the term *foretelling*? What is another example from the Bible in which a prophet foretold something that was going to happen?

2. What comes to mind when you think of the term *forth-telling*? What is another example from the Bible in which a prophet simply proclaimed the truth of God?

....

....

....

....

....

....

....

....

NATURE OF PROPHECY: HONESTY, CONFRONTATION, AND DEFENSE

In the New Testament, we read several accounts of how the disciple Peter functioned in the role of a prophet. These accounts reveal several truths about the nature of the gift of prophecy.

First, the gift of prophecy requires prophets to be honest about themselves and seek correction for their errors. False prophets require truth in others but refuse to confront the truth of their own lives. Genuine prophets, on the other hand, always want the truth of God to reign in their lives just as they demand truth in others. In the Gospel of Luke, we read how Jesus commanded Peter on one occasion to launch into the deep and let down his nets for a catch. Peter reluctantly did so . . . and the result was a net-breaking load of fish. Peter recognized his own doubt in the situation and responded as a genuine prophet would respond: "He fell down at Jesus' knees saying, 'Depart from me, for I am a sinful man, O Lord'" (Luke 5:8).

Second, the gift of prophecy leads people to confront evil, hypocrisy, error, and false conclusions. On the day of Pentecost, the followers of Jesus were accused by onlookers of being drunk with wine. But Peter corrected this false assumption by saying, "Let this be known to you, and heed my words. For these are not drunk, as you suppose, since it is only the third hour of the day. But this is what was spoken by the prophet Joel . . ." (Acts 2:14–16). Peter went on to quote the prophecy from Joel, which lead to approximately 3,000 people receiving salvation.

Third, the gift of prophecy is often voiced as a defense of the church, God's people, God's programs, or God's nature. Genuine prophets are advocates of God's work. They never take credit for what God does but always point to Jesus as Savior, Deliverer, Healer, and Lord. In the book of Acts, we read how Peter and John spoke to a lame man at the Beautiful Gate of the Temple. When the man was miraculously healed, the people began to credit the disciples with the power to heal. But Peter was quick to correct them, saying, "Why look so intently at us, as though by our own power or godliness we had made this man walk? The God of Abraham, Isaac, and Jacob, the God of our fathers, glorified His Servant Jesus . . . And His name, through faith in His name, has made this man strong, whom you see and know" (Acts 3:12–13, 16).

3. How did Peter express his understanding of his condition before Christ (see Luke 5:8)? What does this reveal about the nature of his heart?

4. How might the onlookers have mistakenly credited the disciples with the lame man's healing (see Acts 3:1–10)? Why was Peter so quick to remedy this misunderstanding?

NATURE OF PROPHECY: COURAGE AND REVELATION

As we continue to explore the account of Peter's life told in the book of Acts, we uncover two additional principles as it relates to the gift of prophecy.

First, *the gift of prophecy functions without regard to personal consequences for the prophets.* Genuine prophets see the consequences of wickedness and are more concerned those consequences be averted than they are for their own welfare. Shortly after the healing of the lame man, Peter and John were imprisoned for proclaiming Jesus as the Messiah and told not to teach in the name of Jesus. "But Peter and John answered and said to them, 'Whether it is right in the sight of God to listen to you more than to God, you judge. For we cannot but speak the things which we have seen and heard'" (Acts 4:19–20).

Second, the gift of prophecy reveals the character and motives of others—especially those motives that are deceitful or hypocritical. In the early days of the church, we read how a man named Barnabas sold a piece of land and gave the proceeds to the apostles. A couple named Ananias and Sapphira wanted to do the same—but they decided to hold back some of the proceeds and then lie about it. Peter confronted them, saying, "Why has Satan filled your heart to lie to the Holy Spirit and keep back part of the price of the land for yourself? While it remained, was it not your own? And after it was sold, was it not in your own control? Why have you conceived this thing in your heart? You have not lied to men but to God" (Acts 5:3–4).

5. What motivated Peter to continue preaching the gospel in spite of persecution (see Acts 4:1–22)? What does this motivation reveal about the gift of prophecy?

6. What resulted from Peter's confrontation of Ananias and Sapphira (see Acts 5:1–11)? How did this confrontation influence the body of Christ?

CHARACTERISTICS OF A PROPHET

As you may have concluded from reading about Peter, those who have the motivational gift of prophecy will exhibit certain character traits.

First, genuine prophets are willing to be broken by God so they can be more closely conformed to the likeness of Jesus Christ. We see this in Peter's life after the miraculous catch of fish, when he admitted to Christ that he was a sinful man (see Luke 5:4–8). Later, Peter betrayed Jesus by three times denying that he knew Him. When he recognized his error, he wept bitterly (see Luke 22:54–62). Jesus later restored him (see John 21:15–19), which paved the way for him to receive the power of the Holy Spirit on the Day of Pentecost.

Second, prophets are persuasive and do their utmost to evoke change. Genuine prophets will use whatever means are available to them to argue for the truth. They will have little tolerance for lengthy discussions, group consensus, phased-in changes, or slow processes. We see this in Peter's life when he seized the opportunity on the Day of Pentecost to stand before the onlookers in Jerusalem and deliver the message of the gospel. "And with many other words he testified and exhorted them, saying, 'Be saved from this perverse generation'" (Acts 2:40).

Third, prophets demonstrate a strong dependence on Scripture. Genuine prophets base their understanding of truth on the Word of God. We again see this in Peter on the Day of Pentecost when he quoted from Joel and applied that text to Christ, saying, "Men of Israel, hear these words: Jesus of Nazareth, a Man attested by God to you by miracles, wonders, and signs which God did through Him in your midst . . . whom God raised up, having loosed the pains of death, because it was not possible that He should be held by it" (Acts 2:22, 24).

Fourth, prophets are often bold and direct. Genuine prophets have a deep and abiding commitment to the truth and to the Lord—and this devotion is to the *death*. They may thus come across as being fearless or blunt, for they are only fearful that God will be displeased with them for any hesitancy in confronting a lie. We see this in

Peter's life when he was willing to boldly confront the Jewish religious leaders (see Acts 4:8–12).

Fifth, prophets offer answers that may seem simplistic. Prophets tend to see problems in black-and-white terms, so they often "cut to the chase" in the solutions they offer. They want "bottom-line" facts and are quick to take immediate action. Peter saw Ananias and Sapphira's deception in such black-and-white terms: "You have not lied to men but to God" (Acts 5:4).

7. Based on these characteristics, can you identify someone in your life who demonstrates the gift of prophecy? Do *you* have this gift? Explain.

8. What tends to be your emotional response to someone who has the gift of prophecy? Why is this gift of vital importance to the church when used correctly?

OUR ULTIMATE ROLE MODEL

Prophets are vital for the church, and they are direct in what they say. They are like a strong spice: they give flavor, identity, and direction. Prophets can be effective for the gospel when they are operating under the guidance of the Holy Spirit in humility, love, and peace. But they can be destructive when they are not 100-percent reliant on the Holy Spirit at all times. For this reason, we must pray for those who are prophets to be strong and true to God's Word. Above all, we must test their words against the Word of God and heed what they say when they accurately reveal error or deceit in our midst.

Finally, we must recognize that Jesus was a prophet. He was designated as such by the people of His day. For instance, after Jesus performed the miracle of feeding the 5,000 with five barley loaves and two small fish, the people said of Him, "This is truly the Prophet who is to come into the world" (John 6:14). Jesus is thus the supreme role model for all prophets to follow. He spoke the truth of God always, regardless of circumstances or consequences. Yet He always spoke that truth with love as His motivation, and He always had the cleansing of human hearts and reconciliation with God the Father as His goal.

When we are operating in the motivational gift of the prophet, we must do the same.

9. "But he who prophesies speaks edification and exhortation and comfort to men" (1 Corinthians 14:3). How would you define the terms *edification, exhortation,* and *comfort*? Give practical examples.

10. How does a person exercise the gift of prophecy with the preceding qualifications? What happens when those qualifications are not present?

TODAY AND TOMORROW

Today: A person with the gift of prophecy will
have a passion for truth and God's Word.

Tomorrow: I will ask the Lord to increase my zeal
for His Word this week, whether or not He has given
me the gift of prophecy.

CLOSING PRAYER

Heavenly Father, You are so good to give each of us a gift to use in the body of Christ. You have been so gracious and so good to equip us to serve you. Today, speak to those of us who have the gift of prophecy. Help us to see our opportunity and our responsibility in using this gift. Be present with us as we deal with misunderstandings related to our gift. Help us today to begin to function in this unique gift and always use it to build up and edify those in the church.

NOTES AND PRAYER REQUESTS

Use this space to write any key points, questions, or prayer requests from this week's study.

THE GIFT OF SERVICE

IN THIS LESSON

Learning: What is the gift of service?

Growing: How is this different from Jesus' command to have a servant's heart?

Are you motivated to pursue practical areas of service to others? Are you concerned with the practical and tangible work associated with a project? Do you enjoy doing things with your hands and in association with other people? If so, you may have the gift of service.

The Bible instructs us in a number of ways on how we are to engage in godly service to one another. We are to *be alert* and ask the Holy Spirit to show us what needs we are to meet and how to meet them. We are to *show kindness and consideration* to others as we serve them. We are to *give generously*, while remembering we are not responsible for meeting *all* the needs of others. We are to *be joyful* in our service as we allow the Lord to reveal *different ways* of performing service that might be unusual for us. We are to also to *be available* for service at all times and *see the project through* to its completion.

1. "Whatever you do, do it heartily, as to the Lord and not to men, knowing that from the Lord you will receive the reward of the inheritance; for you serve the Lord Christ" (Colossians 3:23–24). What does it mean to perform a service "as to the Lord"?

2. How does an act of service actually serve Jesus? Why is this distinction important to those who have the gift of service?

NATURE OF SERVICE: AWARENESS, JOY, AND DRIVE

In the New Testament, we find that Timothy—the spiritual son and coworker of the apostle Paul—was a man who had the gift of service. Paul's correspondence with Timothy and regarding him reveal several truths about the nature of this gift.

First, those with the gift of service have an awareness of others people's needs and a desire to meet them. Those with this gift have a heightened sensitivity to others in need and a compassionate heart that can't help but reach out. Their greatest satisfaction comes in seeing a need met, in part or in full, through their efforts. They also have a desire to bring pleasure and joy to others. One manifestation of this desire is usually a great memory concerning the likes and dislikes of other people. People with this gift go far beyond what is required to meet a need. They truly seek to *bless* others, not simply to provide the bare minimum.

Paul wrote this about Timothy: "I trust in the Lord Jesus to send Timothy to you shortly, that I also may be encouraged when I know your state. For I have no one like-minded, who will sincerely care for your state" (Philippians 2:19–20). Paul didn't know anyone who would care for the Philippians with the same tenderness, love, and diligence as Timothy. We also find that Timothy was a man who continually ministered to Paul (see Acts 19:22). Timothy cared for Paul's practical needs and assisted him in every way possible.

Second, those with the gift of service experience true joy in helping others. Those with a gift of service take delight in seeing the accomplishments and success of others and are willing do all the background work that make that happen. They experience a deep sense of satisfaction when they see those whom they are serving doing the work that God has called them to do. On the other hand, they are dismayed when they see those whom they are serving squandering time or devoting energy to things that are unproductive.

Paul wrote to the Corinthians, "For this reason I have sent Timothy to you, who is my beloved and faithful son in the Lord, who will remind you of my ways in Christ, as I teach everywhere in every church" (1 Corinthians 4:17). It is evident that Timothy took great joy in seeing others mature in Christ. Those with the gift of service are likewise generous in giving their time, energy, and effort to worthwhile projects that bring glory to God.

Third, those with the gift of service are driven to meet other people's needs and may overextend their own strength. People with this gift are so concerned about getting the job done they may overlook the passing of time or meeting their own needs. As Paul cautioned Timothy, "No longer drink only water, but use a little wine for your stomach's sake and your frequent infirmities" (1 Timothy 5:23). Paul sent Timothy to minister in Crete—one of the most difficult places to preach the gospel and nurture a group of believers. Timothy no doubt encountered stressful and difficult situations during the course of his ministry on the island. He was so faithful in his service that he evidently neglected his own health.

Another downside for those with the gift of service is that they may be so highly motivated to help others that they overlook the emotional needs of their own family. They often get so wrapped up in meeting the needs of those they see as genuinely "needy" that they neglect the less obvious needs of those around them. They must thus take special care to make sure they are not serving to the point of harming their own health or their relationships.

3. How is the *gift* of service different from the *ministry* of being a servant? How are all Christians called to be servants? How is the gifted person's ministry likely to be unique?

4. Why might it be tempting for a person with the gift of service to think ignoring personal or family needs is commendable? In what ways might it actually be a misuse of that gift?

....

....

....

....

....

....

....

....

....

....

NATURE OF SERVICE: VALIDATION, COMMUNITY, AND ADEQUACY

As we continue to explore the apostle Paul's correspondence related to Timothy, we uncover three additional principles as it relates to the gift of service.

First, those with the gift of service have a need to be appreciated. People with the gift of serving have no desire to waste their time on things that are of no benefit. They are so concerned with the overall success of a project or ministry that they do not want to waste any of their energy on things of little consequence. For this reason, they are motivated when others appreciate their service, because it confirms their ministry is productive, beneficial, and useful. Such affirmation compels them to do even more for the those who are acknowledging them.

Paul was quick to praise Timothy and to acknowledge his efforts. As he wrote to the Corinthians, "If Timothy comes, see that he may be with you without fear; for he does the work of the Lord, as I also do. Therefore let no one despise him" (1 Corinthians 16:10–11).

In working with those who have this gift of service, we must also continually ask, "How can we show appreciation to these individuals who are giving so much of their time, energy, and talents?"

Keep in mind this may lead those with the gift of service to prefer short-range projects. They naturally gravitate toward projects that can be completed in relatively short periods so they can receive this confirmation that their contributions are worthwhile. They tend to get frustrated by long-range projects, so if a project is going to take five years, it should be given to those with the gift of leadership or administration. Those individuals should then recruit those with the gift of service to take on smaller pieces of that project and see them to completion.

Second, those with the gift of service have a strong desire to be with others in community. They are not loners but "people persons." They enjoy being with others because the more people they meet, the more opportunities they have to discover and respond to needs in the lives of others. In the book of Acts, we find that each time Timothy is mentioned, he is typically with someone else. In Acts 19:22, he is mentioned with Erastus. In Acts 20:4, he is part of a team working with Paul that includes Sopater, Aristarchus, Secundus, Gaius, Tychicus, and Trophimus. People with the gift of service find their greatest sense of fulfillment in being with people and relating to them in practical ways. They don't need to see their name in headlines or be in the spotlight, but they do need to be in relationship with others.

Third, those with the gift of service often feel unqualified and inadequate for ministry. They often do not perceive themselves to be ministers— they simply see themselves as practical can-do people. Paul encouraged Timothy in this way on one occasion: "This charge I commit to you, son Timothy, according to the prophecies previously made concerning you, that by them you may wage the good warfare, having faith and a good conscience" (1 Timothy 1:18–19). Timothy may have been discouraged into thinking he was unqualified for the task Paul had given to him. So Paul reminded him of prophecies that confirmed he was doing what God desired him to do, and that he had what it took to engage in successful spiritual warfare.

5. Why does a person who has the gift of service need to hear positive affirmation? How is this different from desiring the praise of others?

....

....

....

....

....

....

....

6. Do you gravitate toward short-term or long-term projects? Do you have long-range vision, or do you tend to notice other service projects that can be immediately fulfilled?

....

....

....

....

....

....

....

FIVE CAUTIONS TO GUARD AGAINST

Those with the gift of service have to be especially sensitive to the following negative aspects of service. *First, they must guard against becoming discouraged if others fail to appreciate their service.* Service should always be undertaken as unto the Lord. People will always disappoint us in their lack of appreciation and will fail to acknowledge our service. But God sees all of our acts, and He is a faithful rewarder of those who serve with diligence and faithfulness.

Second, those with the gift of service must guard against doing so much for others that they never give others an opportunity to give in return. My own mother had a great gift of service. She was so good at anticipating needs in others that she was often halfway finished meeting a need before I had an opportunity to even voice it! Many gifted servants actually feel guilty if they allow others to serve them, yet, ironically, allowing others to serve can be an act of service in itself. For this reason, they must learn to receive from others. If they fail to do so, they will be robbing others of the rewards that come from giving.

Third, those with the gift of service must be sensitive to what God is attempting to teach another person. At times, those gifted in service can be too quick to meet the needs in the lives of others—to the point where they negate the lesson God is trying to convey to them.

Fourth, they must remain attentive to personal spiritual growth and to the disciplines of prayer, praise, and the reading of Scripture. Those with the gift of service must fight the tendency to be so busy with practical tasks that spiritual growth suffers. In the Gospels, we read that Martha was a friend of Jesus and very concerned about serving. Jesus recognized the value of her gift and her service, but he encouraged her in saying, "Martha, Martha, you are worried and troubled about many things. But one thing is needed" (Luke 10:41–42). Jesus called Martha to a time of relaxing in His presence—just listening to Him and enjoying His fellowship.

Fifth, those with the gift of service must avoid the tendency to get sidetracked by more urgent needs. People with the gift of service are quick to notice the needs of others around them—but there can be times when there are more needs than one person can ever hope to meet. Discretion is needed to determine which needs are top priorities. Those with this gift must focus on those tasks that are important and ignore those that are merely urgent.

7. When have you been frustrated by not being allowed to serve another person? How might you have been blessed if your service had been accepted?

8. "Mary has chosen that good part, which will not be taken away from her" (Luke 10:42). What did Jesus mean by "that good part" which Mary had chosen? How had Martha's gift of service actually worked against her at this point?

OUR ULTIMATE ROLE MODEL

One of the names given to Jesus was that of *servant*. As He taught His disciples, "I have given you an example, that you should do as I have done to you. Most assuredly, I say to you, a servant is not greater than his master; nor is he who is sent greater than he who sent him. If you know these things, blessed are you if you do them" (John 13:15–17).

It is important to remember that Jesus said these words to His disciples after He had washed their feet—a lowly task usually done by household servants. As Jesus humbled Himself to serve, so we must humble ourselves to serve. No act of service to another human being should ever be considered too lowly or beneath our dignity.

In employing our gift of service, we must always keep Jesus as our role model. We are to serve in His name, for His glory, and in the same manner of love that He showed to others. Jesus served with a sacrificial heart. He gave His all. He calls those who are given the gift of service to do the same.

9. What did Jesus mean when He said, "A servant is not greater than his master"? In what ways might we consider ourselves better than Jesus when it comes to serving others?

10. What types of service, if any, do you tend to think of as beneath you? When has someone performed such a service for you?

TODAY AND TOMORROW

Today: All Christians are called to be servants, but some have a special gift of serving others.

Tomorrow: I will ask the Lord to teach me how to serve others like Him, whether or not I have the gift of service.

CLOSING PRAYER

Father, thank You for the example of Jesus, who came to this earth not to be served but to serve. You have equipped us to serve in every area of life, regardless our occupation or vocation. And You have provided the means by which we can fulfill that work You have given us—and do it in a way that yields the least amount of weariness, frustration, anxiety, and fear . . . and the greatest amount of contentment, fulfillment, and joy. Thank You for equipping us in a way that enables us to glorify You, honor You, and bring others to an understanding of You.

NOTES AND
PRAYER REQUESTS

Use this space to write any key points, questions, or prayer requests from this week's study.

THE GIFT OF TEACHING

Learning: How can I know if I have
the gift of teaching?

Growing: What are the most important
aspects of being a teacher?

Are you concerned with accuracy when the Word of God is taught? Do you desire to see the truth passed on to the next generation and to those who are lacking in wisdom? Do you wish to see the lives of others changed as a result of information being given to them? If so, you may have the motivational gift of teaching.

Those who have been gifted as teachers are challenged by God's Word to exhibit certain behaviors. First, they exhibit *self-control.*

They are able to focus on the issue that is at hand and avoid detours as they prepare the lesson that they are to teach. Second, they have a *respect for the Word of God*. They seek the truth of Scripture and never approach it with the intent of denying its validity. Third, they are *diligent*. They stick to their research until they have a thorough knowledge of the subject and have prepared the best lesson possible. Finally, they are *dependable*. Others can always rely on them to "rightly divide" the Word of truth.

Those who operate under the guidance of the Holy Spirit and who recognize they are gifted as teachers will not find teaching to be a burden. Rather, these behaviors will be the natural way that they respond to any opportunity to teach. To the person gifted in teaching, there is no greater joy than to study the Bible and then share what has been learned.

1. "With my whole heart I have sought You; oh, let me not wander from Your commandments! Your word I have hidden in my heart, that I might not sin against You" (Psalm 119:10–11). According to these verses, what is required of a person who wants to teach?

2. What role does verbal communication play in teaching others? What role does your own example play? How do the above verses apply to each?

....

....

....

....

....

....

NATURE OF TEACHING: ORDER, ACCURACY, AND DETAILS

One of the foremost teachers in the Bible is Luke. Look at how he begins his Gospel: "Inasmuch as many have taken in hand to set in order a narrative of those things which have been fulfilled among us, just as those who from the beginning were eyewitnesses and ministers of the word delivered them to us, it seemed good to me also, having had perfect understanding of all things from the very first, to write to you an orderly account, most excellent Theophilus, that you may know the certainty of those things in which you were instructed" (Luke 1:1–4).

Luke says that he is an expert, that his understanding is "perfect," and that his account will be orderly. His desire is for Theophilus to "know [with] certainty" or with exactness of detail. In Luke's day, teaching was a highly valued profession in both Jewish and Greek circles. To be a teacher within the early church was an exalted position, and few were called teachers. A great responsibility was thus placed on teachers like Luke to be accurate, wise, diligent in their research, and skilled in their ability to present information.

Then as now, those with the gift of teaching were expected to display certain characteristics. *First, they were to have order in their teaching.* Teachers need to present material so it is easy to follow. Luke notes that he is going to write an orderly "account." Another translation of those words would be "consecutive order." Teachers lay out their material so it all points toward specific themes that convey the main point.

Second, those with the gift of teaching must be concerned with the accuracy of words and the use of language. Teacher are concerned with precise definitions and shades of meaning. This can make them irritating at times to others because they are always asking, "What do you mean by that?" They want to hear and speak with accuracy.

Third, those with the gift of teaching delight in researching and reporting as many details as possible. Those gifted in teaching likewise delight in their own study of Scripture and their own research. They take great joy in seeing meaning in factual details that others might have overlooked. Once this information has been acquired, teachers long to share everything they know. At times, they may provide more information than others want or need to hear—but this is because they feel compelled to "teach all."

Luke includes more details about key events in his Gospel than are found in any of the other Gospels. Luke sees meaning in details. No other Gospel writer tells us about the birth of Jesus as Luke does. He devotes nearly three chapters to the birth of Jesus. He tells not only the story of Mary and Joseph but also the stories of Zacharias, Elizabeth, Simeon, and Anna. He deals with the facts and also with dialogue, monologue, and references to the Old Testament.

3. "[Christ] we preach, warning every man and teaching every man in all wisdom, that we may present every man perfect in Christ Jesus" (Colossians 1:28). What does it mean to "present every man perfect in Christ Jesus"? How is this done?

4. What is the role of the teacher in the above process? What is the role of the teacher's audience?

....

....

....

....

....

....

....

....

....

NATURE OF TEACHING: INTEREST, KNOWLEDGE, AND FACTS

As we continue to explore what the Bible says about teachers, we uncover three additional principles as it relates to this gift.

First, those with the gift of teaching are interested in knowing as much as possible about a subject. Teachers never tire of delving into an area of study or engaging in multiple studies with increasing depth over time. Teachers want all of the information that they present to be accurate, valid, and verifiable. Traditional historical accounts tell us that Luke took several years to research his Gospel. He spoke with numerous people who had known Jesus personally.

Second, those with the gift of teaching desire knowledge and understanding. Those with the gift of prophecy want people to make the right decision and recognize what is at stake if they make the wrong decision. Those with the gift of exhortation are concerned that others understand the step-by-step process necessary to reach a particular goal. Teachers, by comparison, are concerned that others know the Bible and the commandments of God. Acquisition of knowledge is the goal. Luke states he wrote his Gospel so that Theophilus "may know the certainty of those things in which you were instructed" (Luke 1:4).

Third, those with the gift of teaching are primarily concerned with facts, not illustrations or applications. Teachers are rarely impulsive and often reject emotional material or illustrations. They nearly always have a tendency toward logic and organization. They are not likely to delight in lengthy discussion. In fact, they can quickly become irritated with those who talk too much—especially so if those individuals don't know what they are talking about! To this end, teachers develop a method for doing research, determining what is true, and then presenting the information. They sift all things through their method before drawing a conclusion.

5. "Let the word of Christ dwell in you richly in all wisdom, teaching and admonishing one another in psalms and hymns and spiritual songs, singing with grace in your hearts to the Lord" (Colossians 3:16). What does it mean to "let the word of Christ dwell in you richly"? How is this done? What role does wisdom play?

6. What does it mean to "admonish" someone? How is this different from teaching? How do the two work together?

FIVE CAUTIONS TO GUARD AGAINST

The goal for teachers must be to present Jesus to others—with the intent that those individuals grow up in their faith to be more like Christ—and not to convince others of their own intellect. For this reason, teachers must be cautious in how they exercise their gift.

First, they must communicate in a clear and concise manner. All too often, teachers are content to present the facts without making their subject matter of interest to their students. For true learning to occur, teachers must be good researchers and organizers of information—*and* also effective communicators. Those who know how to convey information in a way that will captivate the will and attention of those who hear him speak or read his writing.

Second, teachers must be open to new means of presenting information. Teachers have a tendency to be too narrow in their interpretation of what is information, fact, or knowledge. They see declarative statements as more desirable than telling stories, even though stories are an excellent vehicle for conveying the truth of God's Word. Jesus, of course, was a master at telling *parables*—the use of stories to convey spiritual truth. Most teachers can benefit from incorporating more illustrations and applications into their factual presentations.

Third, teachers must not get hung up small errors in detail but look to the big picture. Teachers may be tempted to dismiss an entire presentation solely on the basis of one particular error. They need to be able to sift error from truth and look at the "big picture." They must be open at all times to have an enlarged vision of what the Lord wants to do in the world today and what role He desires for people to have in that plan.

Fourth, teachers must be open to the intuitive spiritual leading of the Holy Spirit to discern truth. Many teachers rely on their own intellectual abilities and skills to evaluate situations. However, they must also be open to hearing what the Holy Spirit may whisper into their hearts and minds. Truth is more than facts.

Fifth, teachers must never substitute academic degrees for genuine wisdom from God. I have met numerous people who have had very little formal education but who have had a great understanding of both God's Word and the ways in which God works in the human heart. I have also met people who have had a string of degrees behind their names who could barely communicate with sense and who had no understanding of God. Formal education is not a qualifier for the gift of teaching. We must never look down on those who have this genuine motivational gift without formal degrees—and neither must we exalt those who call themselves teachers solely because they have completed degrees but have no gift of God for teaching.

7. Why is it vital for those who have the motivational gift of teaching to be clear in their communication and be open to new ways of presenting information?

8. What problems occur when a teacher gets hung up on small errors, fails to look at the "big picture," and is not open to being led by the Holy Spirit?

OUR ULTIMATE ROLE MODEL

Jesus' disciples frequently addressed Him as "Teacher." Jesus taught by example, by illustration, and by direct presentation of information. Matthew describes Jesus' ministry in his Gospel as one of teaching, preaching, and healing—and in each instance, teaching is the first aspect that is mentioned (see, for example, Matthew 4:23). Jesus' Sermon on the Mount opens with this preface: "Seeing the multitudes, He went up on a mountain, and when He was seated His disciples came to Him. Then He opened His mouth and taught them" (Matthew 5:1–2).

Jesus made a clear statement about the importance of teaching when He said, "Whoever therefore breaks one of the least of these commandments, and teaches men so, shall be called least in the kingdom of heaven; but whoever does and teaches them, he shall be called great in the kingdom of heaven" (Matthew 5:19). Those with the gift of teaching are obligated to personally live by the truth. They must recognize they teach not only with their words but also by the example of their lives. Those who do not are *false* teachers.

Repeatedly in Scripture, we find admonitions to avoid such individuals. Peter wrote, "There will be false teachers among you, who will secretly bring in destructive heresies, even denying the Lord who bought them, and bring on themselves swift destruction. And many will follow their destructive ways, because of whom the way of truth will be blasphemed. By covetousness they will exploit you with deceptive words; for a long time their judgment has not been idle, and their destruction does not slumber" (2 Peter 2:1–3).

Jesus embodied and demonstrated good teaching throughout His life. He even made teaching a part of His great commission to His disciples. Matthew closes his Gospel with this statement from Christ: "Go therefore and make disciples of all nations . . . teaching them to observe all things that I have commanded you" (Matthew 28:19–20). Teaching was vital to Him!

9. Who are the best teachers you have encountered in your life? What made their teaching so effective for you?

10. How did Jesus stress the importance of solid teaching? What tactics do false teachers use to deceive people? How can you identify a false teacher?

TODAY AND TOMORROW

Today: A teacher teaches as much by example as by Word.

Tomorrow: I will diligently examine my own life this week, looking for areas where my actions don't match the teachings of the Word of God.

CLOSING PRAYER

Lord, You have given us clear direction in every aspect of our lives. We thank You today for all of the teachings that You have provided in Your Word. We also thank You for the many admonitions You have provided in Your Word that if we have the motivational gift of teaching, we are to take care in how we operate in this gift. Empower us to dispel the misunderstandings of others and lead them into the knowledge of Your truth. Help us to continue to examine our hearts, look to You, and be willing yield to Your direction as it relates to our spiritual gifts.

NOTES AND
PRAYER REQUESTS

Use this space to write any key points, questions, or prayer requests from this week's study.

THE GIFT OF EXHORTATION

IN THIS LESSON

Learning: What exactly is exhortation?

Growing: How does one use a gift of exhortation in daily life?

Are you concerned about correcting error wherever and whenever you find it? Do you care deeply about helping people avoid mistakes—and helping those who have made mistakes to repent of their ways? If so, you may have the gift of exhortation.

One of the key biblical figures who exemplified the gift of exhortation was the apostle Paul. He wrote, "[Christ] we preach, warning every man and teaching every man in all wisdom, that we may present every man perfect in Christ Jesus. To this end I also labor, striving according to His working which works in me mightily" (Colossians 1:28-29). The word *warning* in this passage can also be translated as *admonishing* or *exhorting*. Exhortation always has an element of caution and concern about it. The exhorter desires to see every believer stay on the straight and narrow path that leads to both heavenly and earthly rewards.

Jesus said, "I tell you the truth. It is to your advantage that I go away; for if I do not go away, the Helper will not come to you; but if I depart, I will send Him to you" (John 16:7). The word translated *Helper* in this verse is the Greek word *Parakletos*, which is the same word used for *exhorter*. Those with the gift of exhortation come alongside other believers to help them understand and adhere to the truth. Those who are genuine *helpers* or *exhorters* encourage others by presence, by word, and by actions to continue in following Christ.

Each of us needs to have at least one person who functions as an exhorter in our lives. This is a person who periodically asks, "What is God doing in your life? What are you doing to develop your relationship with the Lord? How is the Lord working in your life to make you more like Jesus Christ?" Such a person will exemplify the traits of *wisdom, discernment, faith, discretion, love,* and *enthusiasm*. If you allow a person with these qualities to help you as he or she receives guidance from the Holy Spirit, you will be greatly blessed!

1. What does the term *exhort* mean in your own words? What are practical examples of exhortation that you can provide?

2. "For our exhortation did not come from error or uncleanness, nor was it in deceit. But as we have been approved by God to be entrusted with the gospel, even so we speak, not as pleasing men, but God who tests our hearts" (1 Thessalonians 2:3–4). What are some of the qualities of an exhorter? What is required on that person's part?

Nature of Exhortation: Growth, Potential, Concern, and Focus

The Bible reveals several important qualities of those who possess the gift of exhortation. *First, they desire to see others grow in their faith.* Exhorters want to see others growing in their spiritual lives. They are people-oriented, discipleship-oriented, growth-oriented, and maturity-oriented. Exhorters are always quick to ask, "Where are you in your spiritual life?"

Second, those with the gift of exhortation desire to see others discover their spiritual potential. Exhorters do not want others to be anything less than what God has called them to be. They can typically discern the potential in other people and visualize their spiritual achievement. They have insight as to what God might do in and through others if they are willing to yield their talents, abilities, and energy to the Lord. Once exhorters see such potential, they feel compelled to encourage those individuals to reach their potential and turn away from anything that might diminish their growth in Christ.

Third, those with the gift of exhortation are concerned about the spiritual welfare of others. They will do their utmost to find a way of communicating with another person, asking questions and probing until they are satisfied that person is growing in Christ. If exhorters discover an error or blockage in another's growth, they will be quick to point it out and identify the steps that need to be taken for the person to get back on track with the Lord. Like the apostle Paul, they are never hesitant to call out a problem they see in a person's life and then provide practical wisdom from God on how it should be handled.

Exhorters can thus seem aggressive in the eyes of those who are choosing sin or who are apathetic toward growing spiritually. Those who come face to face with exhortation may feel as if they are in the hot seat. However, the goal of exhorters—if they are truly following the lead of the Holy Spirit—is not to produce guilt or shame but to help the person move forward in a personal relationship with the Lord. People with this gift often gravitate toward a career in counseling because they want to see others grow in this manner.

Fourth, those with the gift of exhortation are focused on pointing others toward Christ. Exhorters must always concentrate on the truth of God's Word and the message of God's salvation through Christ. Otherwise, they are merely giving human advice and human wisdom. They identify ways in which others can turn to Christ and to the Holy Spirit, following Jesus Christ as their example, and trusting in the Holy Spirit for daily guidance. We see this focus in Paul's life. His entire theme for the churches was "Christ Jesus in me, and I in Christ Jesus."

3. "And when they had preached the gospel to that city and made many disciples, they returned to Lystra, Iconium, and Antioch, strengthening the souls of the disciples, exhorting them to continue in the faith" (Acts 14:21–22). How would you describe some of the essential traits that a person with the gift of exhortation possesses?

4. How can those who are operating in the gift of exhortation know that they are being led by the Holy Spirit? What must their primary goal and focus always be?

NATURE OF EXHORTATION: INSTRUCTION, VALUE, APPLICATION, AND PRESENCE

As we examine the life and ministry of the apostle Paul, we discover several additional traits that those with the gift of exhortation possess. *First, they are able to give precise instructions about how a person might grow in relationship with Christ.* Exhorters are step-one, step-two, step-three type people who understand the process necessary for people to apply the truth of God's Word to their lives. We see this throughout

Paul's letters, where he offers step-by-step instructions for believers. His arguments are always organized and thought-through so those who read his admonitions can understand clearly what he is saying and desiring on their behalf.

Second, those with the gift of exhortation have learned value in suffering. Exhorters desire to see others avoid suffering and come through hardship victoriously. However, they have also learned that suffering can have great value in breaking old patterns of sin and adopting new patterns of right behavior in a person's life. Paul certainly learned the lessons associated with suffering during the course of his ministry. As he wrote to the Corinthians, "Therefore most gladly I will rather boast in my infirmities, that the power of Christ may rest upon me. Therefore I take pleasure in infirmities, in reproaches, in needs, in persecutions, in distresses, for Christ's sake. For when I am weak, then I am strong" (2 Corinthians 12:9–10).

Third, those with the gift of exhortation are concerned with the application of God's Word. Prophets want to make sure the truth is proclaimed. Teachers want to make sure it is the whole truth and nothing but the truth. But exhorters ask, "How can this be applied to life? What should a person do with this truth?" Paul was always concerned with how a person was to follow Christ and what a person must do to manifest godly behavior and grow in faith.

Fourth, those with the gift of exhortation want to be present with people and see firsthand how they are growing in their faith. Exhorters are usually good at reading body language and facial expressions. We see this trait in the apostle Paul, who wrote again and again to the churches, "I long to be with you," "I can hardly wait to see you again," and "I was so grateful to hear about you from someone who recently was with you." Exhorters delight in being around people who are interested in deepening their spiritual lives. They tend to thus have little patience with those who want only to live superficially.

One of the chief concerns of those who exhort is to resolve conflicts among groups of people. Those with the gift of exhortation therefore do not shy away from relational problems but get right in the middle to help sort them out and bring healing and reconciliation. Paul's writing often focused on how people should relate to one another—including husbands and wives, parents and children, slaves and slave owners, Jews and Greeks, "bonded" and "free." Paul was always concerned with establishing unity in the Body of Christ.

5. "I myself am confident concerning you, my brethren, that you also are full of goodness, filled with all knowledge, able also to admonish one another" (Romans 15:14). What are the prerequisites for being an exhorter? How are these things attained?

6. In what ways is this verse an exhortation to Paul's audience? How might this exhortation lead others to admonish and exhort one another?

FOUR CAUTIONS TO GUARD AGAINST

Those with the gift of exhortation must be cautious in the following areas. *First, they must guard against oversimplifying a problem.* Exhorters should not promise solutions too quickly or give a quick-fix formula. If they do, the person in need is likely to reject the wisdom as too simplistic. This is not to say the solution offered is wrong. Rather, exhorters must deal with others in compassion and lead them through the steps required, one by one.

Second, exhorters must guard against being insensitive. They must emphasize and identify as fully as possible with the person in need. They must attempt to feel what those in need feel and see what they see. They must view the world through the other person's eyes to understand how to help him or her see the truth with greater clarity.

Third, exhorters must guard against being distracted from their main purpose. Exhorters tend to be focused on the growth and maturity of believers. However, they must never lose sight of the importance of leading people to Christ. In this respect, exhorters can be excellent evangelists for Christ if they are willing to see their ministries in the broader terms of leading people from darkness to light.

Fourth, exhorters must be skilled in applying the Word of God within the context of Scripture as a whole. At times, exhorters may be so quick to apply Scripture that they lift a single verse out of context and offer it as a solution. The Bible is as applicable to our lives today as it was to those for whom it was first written, and exhorters must look for meaning and application that spans all cultures and all history. They must see the entire scope of God's truth.

Of course, what is true for an exhorter is true for all Christians. We must *all* become skilled in applying the *whole* of God's Word to our lives, in winning others to Christ, and in leading people from where they are to where God wants them to be. The exhorter is simply one who is gifted in a special way by the Holy Spirit to do this intuitively and responsively.

7. "Beware, brethren, lest there be in any of you an evil heart of unbelief in departing from the living God; but exhort one another daily, while it is called 'Today,' lest any of you be hardened through the deceitfulness of sin" (Hebrews 3:12–13). How can exhortation help people avoid being hardened in sin? How does it help to "undeceive" people?

....

....

....

....

....

....

8. What does it mean to depart from the living God? How does such a thing happen? What role does exhortation play in avoiding this unfortunate circumstance?

....

....

....

....

....

....

OUR ULTIMATE ROLE MODEL

As with all the motivational gifts, Jesus is our role model in the gift of exhortation. Just think about the way Jesus dealt with people in need. He was not a negative person. He never shamed others or belittled them. The only people that He did not encourage were the Pharisees and Sadducees, because they put great burdens of guilt and shame on others.

Recall, for example, how Jesus dealt with a woman who was caught in the act of adultery. Jesus said to the men who accused her,

"He who is without sin among you, let him throw a stone at her first" (John 8:7). When her accusers went away, "being convicted by their conscience" (verse 9), Jesus was left alone with the woman. "He said to her, 'Woman, where are those accusers of yours? Has no one condemned you?' She said, 'No one, Lord.' And Jesus said to her, 'Neither do I condemn you; go and sin no more'" (verses 10–11).

"Neither do I condemn you. Go and sin no more." Those are the hallmark words of the person who exhorts. Forgiveness, admonition not to sin, compassion, an awareness of a person's potential in Jesus Christ—each of these is to be manifested in exhortation and should be at the core of what an exhorter says and does. The exhorter should be quick to say, "I accept you. I love you in Jesus Christ. I believe in who God created you to be and who He is calling you to be. I recognize that you have sinned, but I forgive you. Now, go and sin no more."

9. Why did Jesus forgive the woman caught in adultery? What were her accusers hoping Jesus would do?

10. How did Jesus' response to the woman demonstrate the gift of exhortation? How does an exhorter respond when confronted with sinful behavior?

TODAY AND TOMORROW

Today: An exhorter spurs others on to
become more like Christ.

Tomorrow: I will consciously strive to become
more like Christ in the coming week.

CLOSING PRAYER

Lord God, we praise You for all of the exhortations that You have given to us in Your Word. You are not content to just save us and then leave us where we are—You are continually calling us to pursue a greater and closer relationship with You. Today, we pray that those of us who have the motivational gift of exhortation will use it not to stir up strife but to address real issues that we see in the body of Christ. Let us always express our gifts in love, recognizing that Jesus serves as our ultimate example to follow. Call others to Your truth through our words and actions.

NOTES AND PRAYER REQUESTS

· ·

Use this space to write any key points, questions, or prayer requests from this week's study.

THE GIFT OF GIVING

IN THIS LESSON

Learning: How is the gift of giving different
from regular tithing?

Growing: What role does a giver play in
the body of Christ?

Do you respond to a need by saying, "What can I do to help?" Do you like to provide for ministries in the church and see the results? Do you find you have a good sense of how to manage your money and re-sources so that you can help? If so, you may have the gift of giving.

The Bible instructs us about a number of characteristics that those with this gift will possess. They are *thrifty,* spending their money wisely and not wasting resources that could otherwise be used for ministry. They are *resourceful* and always able to find a way to meet a need, either through their own giving or by motivating the giving of others. They are *contented* with what they have, demonstrate a *give-and-take* mentality in areas where others find it difficult to be flexible, and *cautious* in their investments. They are also *thankful* for what God has given to them and *grateful* when He uses them to meet a need.

The disciple Matthew exemplifies the gift of giving. He was a tax collector—and thus familiar with financial transactions—and has more to say in general about giving than any other New Testament writer. He also offers wise counsel about giving and is the only New Testament author who makes the statement that our giving should be done in secret. Furthermore, he is the only one to address the issue of our *misuse* of money and resources. Matthew records details about gifts brought to Jesus, about Jesus' condemnation of the Pharisees for allowing people to avoid caring for their parents financially, and who tells us what the Pharisees did with the thirty pieces of silver that Judas returned to them after he had betrayed Jesus.

As you look at the Gospel of Matthew, you will find a great deal of information about money, finances, material possessions, and the proper use of your resources.

THREE STATEMENTS ABOUT GIVING

At the outset of our discussion, let me make three general statements about giving. *First, we are to give regardless of our situation in life.* Giving is not a ministry or motivational gift that is limited to those who are wealthy. Financial status has nothing to do with the gift of giving. Those with this gift will desire to give regardless of the size of their bank account or the possessions they have. They will delight in giving and find satisfaction in doing so.

Second, all of us are commanded to give—and to do so with liberality. All believers are to give tithes faithfully and be generous in their offerings. However, those with the gift of giving "live to give." They cannot help but give at every opportunity . . . and they are generally as quick to give as much as they can as often as they can. Yet we must never just leave the giving to those who have this gift. Each of us is to give as God commands.

Third, giving is not limited to money. A gift may be material resources, time, talent, energy, or creativity. However, regardless of the form it takes, it will be one that has value and produces a material benefit. Givers may volunteer their time, talent, and energy to a particular cause, knowing their effort will produce a tangible blessing to others. Again, we all are to give in many ways, but those with the gift of giving are eager to give in every way possible.

1. "But this I say: He who sows sparingly will also reap sparingly, and he who sows bountifully will also reap bountifully" (2 Corinthians 9:6). What does it mean to sow *sparingly* or *bountifully*? How can you know if your gift is sparing or bountiful?

2. Why do you think Paul uses the metaphor of planting and harvesting when discussing the topic of giving? How is giving similar to gardening?

Nature of Giving: Wisdom, Humility, and Encouragement

There are several key characteristics that those with the gift of giving will possess. *First, they have a keen ability to make wise investments and purchases in order to have more money to give.* Many people are bargain hunters and wise investors. However, the person with the gift of giving seeks to save and invest *in order to have more to give.* Many bargain hunters desire to save money so they can spend the savings on themselves, but the person who is a giver desires to spend the savings on the work of the Lord.

Second, those with the gift of giving desire to give humbly and not call attention to themselves. People with the gift of giving are not motivated by applause or public recognition. Rather, they find their satisfaction simply in making the gift. In fact, their total emphasis is on meeting the need, not on having others acknowledge that they have met the need. They take Jesus' words to heart when He taught, "Do not do your charitable deeds before men, to be seen by them. Otherwise you have no reward from your Father in heaven. Therefore, when you do a charitable deed, do not sound a trumpet before you as the hypocrites do in the synagogues and in the streets, that they may have glory from men" (Matthew 6:1–2).

Third, those with the gift of giving are eager to encourage others to give. Those with the gift of giving desire so greatly to see a need met that they will challenge others around them—regardless of their financial situation—to give what they can. They also recognize the value of giving and understand there is a cycle to giving that includes receiving. The giving-receiving-giving-receiving cycle is motivating and rewarding to those who have this gift.

3. "Command those who are rich in this present age not to be haughty, nor to trust in uncertain riches but in the living God, who gives us richly all things to enjoy. Let them do good, that they

be rich in good works, ready to give, willing to share, storing up for themselves a good foundation for the time to come, that they may lay hold on eternal life" (1 Timothy 6:17–19). What might cause a wealthy person to become haughty? According to these verses, how does this attitude demonstrate faulty thinking?

4. Good works do not bring salvation, so what did Paul mean when he said, "that they may lay hold on eternal life"? How is godly giving a way of holding onto things of eternity?

NATURE OF GIVING: DISCERNMENT, STEWARDSHIP, REJOICING, AND QUALITY

As we continue to explore what the Bible has to say about giving, we discover four additional characteristics that those with the motivational gift of giving will possess. *First, they often have an ability to discern financial and material needs that others overlook.* They are quick to calculate how much is needed, when it will be needed, and the how resources might best be applied to meeting the need. They take to heart Jesus' teaching, "What profit is it to a man if he gains the whole world, and is himself destroyed or lost?" (Luke 9:25).

Second, those with the gift of giving regard stewardship over material possessions and finances as indicative of a person's ability to be a good steward of spiritual matters. They take Jesus at His word when He said, "He who is faithful in what is least is faithful also in much; and he who is unjust in what is least is unjust also in much" (Luke 16:10). Givers are concerned about good stewardship, so they may live frugally and modestly—even if they have great financial wealth. Furthermore, they are often unrecognized because they are unpretentious in what they possess and use. They are not motivated to accumulate things but rather to use things to benefit others. They desire to gain wealth only so they can give it away.

Third, those with the gift of giving rejoice when their giving is an answer to someone else's prayer. Givers delight in being the tools the Lord has used in another person's life. They rejoice because they have assurance that they heard correctly from the Lord. They rejoice that a legitimate need has been met. They rejoice that the faith of another person has been activated and built up. They always want to be right on target when it comes to sensing needs and responding as the Lord leads.

Fourth, those with the gift of giving desire to give gifts of high quality. They do not look for the cheapest or most meager way to meet a need. Rather, they wants to give in abundance and quality, just as the Lord has given to them in abundance and quality. They then take joy in being a part of the ministry of the person to whom they have given. When they make a material gift, they feels as if they are giving of themselves. They feel personally invested in the life of the person to whom they have given. Being part of that person's success brings them joy.

5. "Let each one give as he purposes in his heart, not grudgingly or of necessity; for God loves a cheerful giver" (2 Corinthians 9:7). When have you received a gift that was given grudgingly? How did the giver's attitude influence your perception of the gift?

6. When have you received a gift of high cost or quality that was given cheerfully? How did the giver's joy influence your perception of the gift?

FIVE CAUTIONS TO GUARD AGAINST

As with the other motivational gifts that we have discussed in this study, there are several cautions for those with the gift of giving to take to heart. *First, givers must never become so overly concerned with material goods that they neglect the spiritual dimension of their lives.* Givers need to maintain balance in this area to ensure they engage in the practices that will continue to build their relationship with the Lord—including prayer, Bible reading, and personal study.

Second, givers must never attempt to control the ministry or life of another person through their gifts. At times, those who give are concerned with making certain their gift is used in a proper way. However, those who give must learn how to release their gifts to the work of God and trust that others will properly manage and administer those resources.

Third, givers must never pressure others to give as generously as they do. Givers tend to be turned off by high-pressure tactics, preferring instead to respond to simple requests from those who are in need. As Jesus said, "Give to him who asks you, and from him who wants to borrow from you do not turn away" (Matthew 5:42). However, just as givers tend to reject such tactics, they must be careful not to engage in these high-pressure tactics themselves.

Fourth, givers must never become stingy to their own families. Those who are intensely concerned about the needs of others often overlook the needs of their spouses and children. Legitimate needs of family members should be met.

Fifth, givers must always remember to be thankful for what they receive. Givers are often so focused on their own giving that they rebuff or fail to acknowledge the things that they are given by others. Givers need to recognize the gifts of others and encourage them.

7. "Heal the sick, cleanse the lepers, raise the dead, cast out demons. Freely you have received, freely give" (Matthew 10:8).

Notice this list of gifts does not include money. How can a person with the gift of giving bless others without spending money?

8. What gifts has the Lord given you—both spiritually and materially? How can you demonstrate your gratitude for those gifts?

OUR ULTIMATE ROLE MODEL

Jesus, of course, is our role model for sacrificial and joyful giving. No person has ever given as much as He gave, for He gave His *very life on the cross* so that we might have eternal life. Jesus taught His disciples, "Greater love has no one than this, than to lay down one's life for his friends" (John 15:13). Jesus willingly gave His life in obedience to His father. As we read in perhaps the most famous verse in the New Testament: "For God so loved the world that He gave His only begotten Son, that whoever believes in Him should not perish but have everlasting life" (John 3:16). Those who have the gift of giving have a tremendous opportunity to be like Jesus and bless others in the Body of Christ. They should seek to continually encourage others in the proper use of finances to make the extension of the gospel possible.

9. "For where your treasure is, there your heart will be also" (Luke 12:34). What are some real-life examples of where you have seen this principle at work? Why does a person's treasure influence his or her heart?

10. Where is *your* treasure? What do you value most in life? How is this influencing your daily decisions and actions?

TODAY AND TOMORROW

Today: All Christians are called to give generously, but the gift of giving enables a person to meet needs that otherwise would be missed.

Tomorrow: I will look for opportunities this week to meet the needs of others, as the Lord leads.

CLOSING PRAYER

Heavenly Father, You have given us so much! You have given us the Words and principles that bring life—that allow us to live happily, joyfully, peacefully, and contentedly. Today, we pray that we would be a reflection of You and give to others. For those of us who operate in this motivational gift, we pray that You will show us new areas of need and ways that we can help those who are struggling. You are our Shepherd, and in You we lack nothing. So let us be cheerful givers so we can let others know of all the abundant blessings You provide.

NOTES AND
PRAYER REQUESTS

Use this space to write any key points, questions, or prayer requests from this week's study.

THE GIFT OF ORGANIZATION

IN THIS LESSON

Learning: If Christ is the head of the church, why do we need gifted leaders?

Growing: How can a person recognize the gift of leadership?

Are you uncomfortable in a leaderless group? Do you feel restless or frustrated if things are disorderly? If so, you may have the motivational gift of organization. This gift is sometimes called the gift of leading, ruling, or the gift of administration. The Greek word used in the New Testament literally means "the one who stands out front."

The Bible reveals several qualities that those who have the gift of organization need to possess. They need to be *organized* in their thinking and exhibit *orderliness* to others. They do not *delay* in taking actions and are willing to assume *responsibility* for all aspects of a project or group endeavor. They demonstrate *humility* by recognizing that others must be part of the team if the job is to be done. They are *determined* in reaching their goal and *loyal* to God and others in authority—as well as to those who are following their leadership. Godly leaders regard themselves as under the authority of the Holy Spirit. Ungodly leaders are tyrants to be avoided.

Often, the gift of organization is undervalued, as those who possess it do not stand out as much as individuals with the gift of teaching, exhortation, or prophecy. Yet organizers are no less spiritual than those with the other gifts. In fact, to the Christian, *all things* are spiritual. There is no distinction before God between secular life and spiritual life—*everything* has a spiritual foundation. Organizers are "spiritual dreamers in action." They see the intended design of God and turn it into reality. They engage in major undertakings to turn the will of God into a reality on earth. They can visualize the result that God desires and make it happen.

ORDER IN THE EARLY CHURCH

In the book of Acts, we read of problems that arose in the early church in Jerusalem regarding the distribution of food. Many of the believers had pooled their earthly resources and were meeting together daily for fellowship, for study of the Word, and for eating meals. However, "there arose a complaint against the Hebrews by the Hellenists, because their widows were neglected in the daily distribution" (Acts 6:1). In other words, some of the members of the church were being neglected, while others were indulging themselves. As you read the following account of what happened, note how organization was linked to spiritual concerns, and how organization created a climate in which spiritual fruit was produced.

Then the twelve summoned the multitude of the disciples and said, "It is not desirable that we should leave the word of God and serve tables. Therefore, brethren, seek out from among you seven men of good reputation, full of the Holy Spirit and wisdom, whom we may appoint over this business; but we will give ourselves continually to prayer and to the ministry of the word."

And the saying pleased the whole multitude. And they chose Stephen, a man full of faith and the Holy Spirit, and Philip, Prochorus, Nicanor, Timon, Parmenas, and Nicolas, a proselyte from Antioch, whom they set before the apostles; and when they had prayed, they laid hands on them. Then the word of God spread, and the number of the disciples multiplied greatly in Jerusalem, and a great many of the priests were obedient to the faith (verses 2–7).

This example serves to further illustrate that organization is not counterproductive to the work of the Holy Spirit and should not be viewed as "less spiritual" than the other gifts. The Holy Spirit desires order, and when the ministry gift of organization is strong and Spirit-led in a group, all other ministry gifts flourish. The gospel is preached, souls are saved, and the church grows and develops even greater strength.

1. What motivated the apostles to find people with the gift of organization? How did Stephen and others help the twelve to carry out their own ministries more effectively?

2. What sort of things did Stephen and the others do for the body of Christ? What did their gift of organization look like?

....

....

....

....

....

....

ORDERLY AND EFFECTIVE WORKS

Another individual in the New Testament who exhibited the gift of organization was James. According to historians, he was known as "James the Just" or "James the Righteous" due to his virtue. In the book of Acts, we read how James served as the leader of the early Jerusalem church and presided over "the Jerusalem Council," which was tasked with resolving the issue of whether Gentile converts had to accept Jewish practices to be considered Christians.

James led the council with wisdom in this regard, ultimately ruling, "I judge that we should not trouble those from among the Gentiles who are turning to God, but that we write to them to abstain from things polluted by idols, from sexual immorality, from things strangled, and from blood" (Acts 15:19–20). Later, he penned the letter in the New Testament that bears his name. Many people, after reading this letter, conclude that James is being too practical and not spiritual enough—that he emphasizes works as being of equal importance to faith.

However, we must take care not to misunderstand James. He regards faith very highly and sees no substitute for it, but he is also very concerned that faith be put to work in an orderly and effective way. Throughout his epistle, we find a strong admonition that we should be "doers of the word and not hearers only" (James 1:22).

In fact, James says that if we are *hearers only and not doers*, we have deceived ourselves.

In James's own words: "For if anyone is a hearer of the word and not a doer, he is like a man observing his natural face in a mirror; for he observes himself, goes away, and immediately forgets what kind of man he was. But he who looks into the perfect law of liberty and continues in it, and is not a forgetful hearer but a doer of the work, this one will be blessed in what he does" (James 1:23–25). James had great practical concern for orderliness and diligence!

3. Suppose you discovered something embarrassing on your face or clothing after looking into a mirror, but decided to just walk away and not fix it. How is this a good picture of *knowing* God's Word but failing to put it into *practice*?

4. "If a brother or sister is naked and destitute of daily food, and one of you says to them, 'Depart in peace, be warmed and filled,' but you do not give them the things which are needed for the body, what does it profit? Thus also faith by itself, if it does not have works, is dead" (James 2:15–17). When have you known of someone else's desperate need but failed to do anything about it? When has that happened to you?

NATURE OF THE GIFT
OF ORGANIZATION

Those who have the gift of organization bear the following twelve characteristics. *First, they have an ability to see the "big picture."* Leaders and organizers have a capacity to dream big and to believe that God desires to do something more than presently exists.

Second, they have an ability to break down large projects into bite-sized pieces. They are able to break down long-range goals into a sequence of short-range goals.

Third, they are self-starters. They are motivated to accomplish the goals that are before them. They take great joy in seeing the pieces of the larger puzzle fall into place one-by-one.

Fourth, they are keenly aware of all the resources necessary for accomplishing a goal. The minute they see the goal that God has set before them, they begin to analyze all that is necessary for accomplishing it. They envision ways that the resources might be acquired.

Fifth, they are confident that God-given goals can be accomplished. They are can-do people and have little tolerance for those with objections, unfounded concerns, and a negative or pessimistic outlook.

Sixth, they know how to delegate. They know that they cannot do it all and are willing to relinquish both authority and responsibility so that others can be successful in understanding and completing part of the larger goal. They know how to seek out the right people to undertake various parts of the task that lies ahead.

Seventh, they will often have little tolerance for details. Too many details will simply bog down those individuals who possess the gift of organization!

Eighth, they are able to receive criticism without crumbling. As mentioned earlier, the literal meaning of the Greek word for ruling or leading is "the one who stands out front." Those who are out front are on the firing line—they are the ones most likely to be criticized, questioned, blamed, and misunderstood. They thus have to have skin as thick as a rhinoceros. If they are to accomplish God's plan, they must not allow criticism to deter them.

Ninth, they know their coworkers are loyal and committed to the task at hand. Those who lead expect loyalty from others. They are so loyal to God and so committed to obeying Him that they have no tolerance for anyone who is disloyal or wavering in his or her commitment.

Tenth, they have a tendency to move into a leadership role if no leader emerges or if a situation becomes disorderly. They simply cannot sit idly on the sidelines if they perceive that nobody is moving into a leadership role. Because of this tendency, those with this gift can often be misinterpreted as being egotistical or over-aggressive. In truth, these individuals are simply moving to establish order where they perceive disorder exists.

Eleventh, they want to see a goal reached as quickly as possible, as well as possible, and with as few resources as possible. They abhor wasting time, money, talent, or energy.

Twelfth, they delight in seeing projects accomplished. They are not motivated by making money, working with people, or receiving applause but by seeing the *task accomplished* in a way that is pleasing to God. They need few rewards other than the deep satisfaction in knowing that God is pleased and that good work has been done.

5. When have you seen someone arrive on the scene and confidently take the lead on a project? What gifts did that person have which made the project flow more smoothly?

6. "Having then gifts differing according to the grace that is given to us, let us use them . . . he who teaches, in teaching . . . he who gives, with liberality; he who leads, with diligence" (Romans 12:6-8). Why is diligence necessary in the gift of leadership? How is it the equivalent of the giver who gives with liberality or the teacher who teaches?

....

....

....

....

....

....

THREE CAUTIONS TO GUARD AGAINST

Those with the motivational gift of organization must be aware of several negative tendencies. *First, they must take the time to rest and reflect.* Those with this gift are rarely without a project to finish. And as soon as they complete one project, they are eager to move on to the next one. However, God did not create us to be "all work and no play." Rather, we read in the Bible that He made the Sabbath for us to rest physically, emotionally, and spiritually—to relax in His presence and allow Him to rejuvenate us from the inside out.

Second, those with the gift of organization must be cautious to not drive others beyond the limits of their abilities. Those with this gift are highly motivated and can drive others without regard for their capacity, other commitments, or personal limitations. They must be sensitive to the fact that others may not be as motivated, energetic, or insightful as they are.

Third, those with the gift of organization need to avoid relying on their own abilities rather than trusting God to guide priorities. Those with this gift are so capable that they often run ahead of God's timetable or to fail to ask Him, "Are we doing what You want us to do? Are we doing this in the way that You want us to do it? Do we have our priorities straight?"

7. "Let no one despise your youth, but be an example to the believers in word, in conduct, in love, in spirit, in faith, in purity" (1 Timothy 4:12). How are leaders to serve as an example to those who follow them? What happens when they fail to do this?

8. "Come now, you who say, 'Today or tomorrow we will go to such and such a city, spend a year there, buy and sell, and make a profit'; whereas you do not know what will happen tomorrow. For what is your life? It is even a vapor that appears for a little time and then vanishes away. Instead you ought to say, 'If the Lord wills, we shall live and do this or that'" (James 4:13–15). What attitude is James encouraging in all believers? How might this attitude be difficult for someone with the gift of leadership?

Our Ultimate Role Model

As with all the ministry gifts, Jesus is our role model for the proper use of the gift of organization. In this Gospel, we find that He referred to Himself as the Shepherd of His flock (see John 10:11). He organized His disciples by choosing twelve and then sending them out two by two (see Mark 6:7). He was certainly delegating authority when He gave His disciples this commandment: "Go into all the world and preach the gospel to every creature" (Mark 16:15). Paul had this to say about Jesus' role as the leader of the church: "He put all things under His feet, and gave Him to be head over all things to the church, which is His body, the fullness of Him who fills all in all" (Ephesians 1:22–23).

We all are to be orderly in the way that we conduct our lives. However, those with the ministry gift of organization find great satisfaction in being organized and in seeing the work done, tasks accomplished, and projects completed. They believe that whatever they do, they should "do it heartily, as to the Lord and not to men" (Colossians 3:23). They enjoy work and are likely to be working every day of their lives. We should all be grateful for this gift!

9. What are some examples of godly leadership from the life and ministry of Jesus? What principles of leadership can you glean from His example?

10. When was Jesus also a follower? What can all Christians learn from His example about being a godly follower?

_____

_____

_____

_____

_____

_____

_____

TODAY AND TOMORROW

Today: A godly leader is first and foremost
a godly follower of Christ.

Tomorrow: I will consciously work at being a godly follower
this week, whether or not I have the gift of leadership.

CLOSING PRAYER

Father, Your Word tells us You are a God of order. You are a God who doesn't leave us wandering but leads us along the course that You have set for our lives. Today, we pray that You will continue to call up leaders in Your church with the motivational gift of organization. Raise up a new generation of believers in Christ who will capture Your vision, be willing to step forward and assume responsibility, and know the steps to take to see Your purpose fulfilled. Reveal if this is the gift we have in our own lives so we can take action today.

NOTES AND
PRAYER REQUESTS

Use this space to write any key points, questions, or prayer requests from this week's study.

THE GIFT OF MERCY

Learning: How is the gift of mercy
different from loving others?

Growing: What role does mercy have
in the body of Christ?

Do you have a heart for people? Do you have a desire to see people love one another to a greater degree? If so, you probably have the gift of mercy.

The Bible reveals several traits that those with the gift of mercy will typically possess. They are *attentive* and watch over those who are in need or trouble. They are *sensitive* to needs in others, even without that other person having to say anything. They demonstrate *impartiality* and are *compassionate*. They tend to be *gentle, soft-spoken,* and *yielding* to the wishes of others so harmony and peace might prevail.

They are also willing to *sacrifice* and even endure *suffering* if, in the end, it leads to helping another person.

As with the other motivational gifts, we are all called to bear the fruit of the Spirit, and gentleness is one of the traits identified as such fruit (see Galatians 5:22–23). Yet those with the gift of mercy do not have to say, "I should be merciful in this situation. I must speak kind words and deal with this person gently." Instead, the response of mercy and kindness is immediate and automatic. They *seek out* those who are hurting so they can show mercy.

Jesus said, "Love your enemies, do good, and lend, hoping for nothing in return; and your reward will be great, and you will be sons of the Most High. For He is kind to the unthankful and evil. Therefore be merciful, just as your Father also is merciful" (Luke 6:35–36). Nothing is as fulfilling to those with the gift of mercy as having the opportunity to fulfill this command. They desire to comfort those who are hurting and defending those individuals who seem to be outcast, downtrodden, or treated unfairly by the rest of society.

1. "But the fruit of the Spirit is love, joy, peace, longsuffering, kindness, goodness, faithfulness, gentleness, self-control" (Galatians 5:22–23). How do these verses apply to a person with the gift of mercy? How do they apply to all Christians?

2. How have you seen God demonstrate His kindness to you? How can this help you extend kindness and mercy toward others?

MERCY IN THE BODY OF CHRIST

One person in the New Testament who exemplifies the gift of mercy is the apostle John. He wrote more about love than any of the other Gospel authors: the love of God, Jesus' commandments to love one another, and extensive admonitions to the early believers about love. John valued love so highly the he referred to himself as the one "whom Jesus loved" (John 13:23). John clearly believed that being loved by Jesus was the highest reward and most meaningful mark of identification for a disciple of Christ.

John wrote a great deal about the need for love in the body of Christ. He always saw love as an *action*, not as an emotion. He related love to *Christ*, who truly is our source of love. Without Him, it is impossible for a person truly to love unconditionally. We see this in his first epistle, where he states, "Beloved, let us love one another, for love is of God. . . . God has sent His only begotten Son into the world, that we might live through Him. In this is love, not that we loved God, but that He loved us and sent His Son to be the propitiation for our sins. Beloved, if God so loved us, we also ought to love one another" (1 John 4:7, 9–11).

Often, men think of mercy as a feminine gift. Yet John reveals it is neither feminine nor masculine. He certainly was not the least bit effeminate. Jesus referred to him and his brother as the "Sons of Thunder" (Mark 3:17), yet John was tenderhearted and merciful. Mercy is a character quality that every single person in the body of Christ is to manifest. However, those who bear the gift of mercy find a special purpose in extending grace to others. They are a source of joy in any church, and everyone enjoys having them around. We can readily understand why. After all, who fails to respond to unconditional love and mercy?

3. "If someone says, 'I love God,' and hates his brother, he is a liar; for he who does not love his brother whom he has seen, how can he love God whom he has not seen? And this commandment we have from Him: that he who loves God must love his brother also" (1 John 4:20–21). What does it mean to love your brother? Who is your brother?

4. In what sense is it a lie to say you love God if you don't also love your brother? Why can't a person love others without loving God first?

NATURE OF THE GIFT OF MERCY

Those who have the gift of mercy will bear the following qualities. *First, they have an ability to feel the joy or distress of others.* They have a heightened sense of discernment regarding emotions. They rarely have to ask how someone is doing, because they sense how that person is doing emotionally. They are usually more concerned with inner hurts than outer material or physical needs. They are especially drawn to those who are lonely, fearful, or troubled.

Second, those with the gift of mercy are able to identify with others and vicariously experience what they are going through. They have a special empathy and understanding of those who are under emotional stress, and they are actively attracted to those individuals. They have a great desire to help others by their presence and friendship. They can "rejoice with those who rejoice, and weep with those who weep" (Romans 12:15).

Third, those with the gift of mercy desire to alleviate hurt in others. They see virtually no benefit in pain, suffering, distress, or sorrow. For this reason, they may clash at times with those who have the gift of exhortation, who are able to see benefit in suffering. They must therefore be willing to allow the gift of exhortation to function fully, just as the person with the gift of exhortation must be patient and kind toward the person who has a gift of mercy. Those with other ministry gifts may reach out to hurting individuals with words and material blessing, but the person with the gift of mercy is likely to reach out with open arms.

Fourth, those with the gift of mercy are sensitive to statements and actions that may hurt others. They intuitively feel the pain on behalf of others. They often react harshly if their friends or family members are rejected or hurt in any way. They may respond in a defensive and even angry way if they sense that a person is doing something that may injure someone they love. They are very sensitive to criticism of others.

Fifth, those with the gift of mercy have an ability to sense unconditional love and detect expressions of love that are insincere or hypocritical. They have a greater ability to be wounded themselves, so they are highly vulnerable to feeling emotional pain. Part of their ability to empathize with another person's pain grows out of their own experience.

Sixth, those with the gift of mercy have a great need for friendship. They desire to be in relationships that are marked by commitment and steadfastness. They do not have a high tolerance, however, for friends who manifest a critical spirit.

Finally, those with the gift of mercy are reluctant to speak against any person, regardless of what he or she has done. The danger, of course, is that they may not speak up in times when they *should* confront evil. Mercy must always be balanced with justice. God is always merciful, but it is equally true that God is always just.

5. "Let all bitterness, wrath, anger, clamor, and evil speaking be put away from you, with all malice. And be kind to one another, tenderhearted, forgiving one another, even as God in Christ forgave you" (Ephesians 4:31–32). How would you define *bitterness, wrath, clamor, evil speaking,* and *malice?*

6. What does it mean to be tenderhearted? How is this done?

....

....

....

....

....

....

FIVE CAUTIONS TO GUARD AGAINST

Those with the motivational gift of mercy must continually guard against several negative tendencies. *First, they must avoid being emotional to the point of losing sight of the greater purposes of God.* Those with the gift of mercy must always maintain an objective awareness that God's purposes and God's methods are higher than those of humans—and that God may at times break a person in order to refashion him or her.

Second, they must guard against being weak and indecisive. Those with this gift have a tendency to express tenderness and acceptance rather than firmness and resoluteness for the truth of God. The merciful person must choose to stand strong in the face of evil.

Third, they must guard against being too quick to draw conclusions in defense of those who are being hurt. Those with this gift must not be too impulsive in showing mercy.

Fourth, they must guard against being too forward in their desire to minister to others with their presence, forgiveness, and kindness. Those with this gift must be sensitive to know when they are too close for another person's comfort.

Fifth, they must be cautious that acts of mercy and love do not cross a line. Those with the gift of mercy are wise to extend their gift to those of the same sex, as those who receive mercy from a person of the opposite sex may misinterpret it as an act of romantic love. The gift of mercy is rooted in love. It is thus difficult for some people to maintain proper bounds when showing mercy to those of the opposite sex.

7. "Holy and beloved, put on tender mercies, kindness, humility, meekness, longsuffering; bearing with one another, and forgiving one another" (Colossians 3:12–13). How would you define *tender mercies, humility, meekness,* and *longsuffering*?

8. Notice these qualities of love are associated with forgiving others. Why is this Paul's focus concerning love? What does this teach about the gift of mercy?

Our Ultimate Role Model

Jesus was the embodiment of God's love. He was God's "only begotten son" (John 3:16), sent to this world as an expression of God's infinite love for humankind. Jesus always acted in a merciful way to people in need. He saw and responded to inner needs as much as to their outer material or physical needs. His desire and goal was for people to be reconciled to God the Father and experience His forgiveness and unconditional love.

John tells us, "God did not send His Son into the world to condemn the world, but that the world through Him might be saved" (3:17). Jesus did not merely talk about love or command others to love. Rather, He expressed love in the most merciful way: by giving His own life for the sins of the world. As John also wrote, "By this we know love, because He laid down His life for us. And we also ought to lay down our lives for the brethren" (1 John 3:16).

In any body of believers, there are likely to be more people who feel they have the gift of mercy than any other ministry gift. I believe this is actually healthy for the church. If the church is to be a family, then love, kindness, tenderness, forgiveness, and mercy must be freely flowing. Any body of believers characterized by mercy is going to be healthy. Those who show mercy are going to provide a spiritually helpful balance to those who have other ministry gifts. The gift of mercy certainly balances other gifts, like the gift of prophecy. In situations in which prophets may wound with their sharp denunciation of evil and their strong call to righteousness, the person with a gift of mercy is there to "bandage" the wounded.

9. "Therefore be imitators of God as dear children. And walk in love, as Christ also has loved us and given Himself for us, an offering and a sacrifice to God for a sweet-smelling aroma" (Ephesians 5:1–2). Why did Paul command us to be imitators "as dear children"? How does a child imitate his or her father? How can this help you imitate God's love?

10. What does it mean to "walk in love"? How is this done? How is "walking" more active and deliberate than "standing"? How does this relate to loving others?

TODAY AND TOMORROW

Today: All Christians are called to love one another, but the gift of mercy goes the extra mile in that love.

Tomorrow: I will ask God to help me love others selflessly this week and will seek to show mercy to those who need it.

CLOSING PRAYER

Lord Jesus, thank You for extending to us Your mercy. Thank You for the ultimate act of mercy You demonstrated when You chose to sacrifice Your life so that we could receive salvation from our sins. Help us today to extend that same mercy to others. Today, we pray that those of us who have the motivational gift of mercy will be willing to set up and act on the needs that we see. Our prayer today is that we will become the answer to another person's need.

NOTES AND
PRAYER REQUESTS

. . . .

Use this space to write any key points, questions, or prayer requests
from this week's study.

GIFTED FOR SERVICE

Learning: What is the purpose for my spiritual gifts?

Growing: How will I use my spiritual gifts to both serve others and glorify God?

One of the greatest tragedies in life is for people to live without any sense of purpose. Whether they have a good job or a bad job, their lives are built on nothing more than simply existing from day to day, week to week, and year to year. They don't accomplish anything worthwhile, and they have no desire to do so. This is a tragedy when it is true of any person. But it's especially tragic when a follower of Jesus lives that kind of life. We are meant for much more.

We have talked a lot about gifts throughout this study, but we have not talked much about *purpose*. And we need to talk about purpose, because there is a reason why God has blessed His followers with spiritual gifts. We are not to simply collect these gifts and keep them up on a shelf somewhere. Rather, we are to use them to serve others.

Peter pointed out this truth when he wrote, "As each one has received a gift, minister it to one another, as good stewards of the manifold grace of God" (1 Peter 4:10). Notice first that Peter says, "each one." He is not talking about the collective body of Christ but about individual Christians. Next, he says, "has received." Each follower of Jesus "has received a gift." The verb tense used in this verse means something that happened in the *past*. We have seen that about spiritual gifts—we receive them when we trust Jesus as our Savior and the Holy Spirit begins to work in us. This means if you are a follower of Jesus, you have a spiritual gift. You *received* it.

Finally, Peter says that we are to take our gift and "minister it." This seems like a strange way to say it, but it means we are to *use* those gifts. We are to activate them. Where do we minister our gifts? "To one another." We are commanded to use our spiritual gifts to serve others, which means serving our fellow Christians in the church and serving those outside the church. When we do this, we are "good stewards" of the gifts God has given us.

This is what we will explore in this lesson: the critical importance of knowing the purpose for our spiritual gifts, which is actively using them to serve others.

1. What has surprised you so far in this study? Why?

2. What comes to mind when you think about your purpose or mission in life?

....

....

....

....

....

....

Spiritual Gifts Are for the Common Good

One of the confusing things about this whole idea of spiritual gifts is the word *gift* itself. Gifts are usually something we receive as individuals for our own benefit. For instance, when I get a Christmas gift from my children, I know the gift is for *me*. I receive it. I unwrap it. I open it. I enjoy it. I write the thank-you note on behalf of myself alone. It's *my* gift.

However, spiritual gifts are different, because they are given for the common good. I have the spiritual gift of exhortation, but I didn't receive that gift for myself. I don't use it to benefit myself (though I do enjoy the privilege of preaching) but to benefit the body of Christ. I use it for the common good of God's people.

Paul said it this way: "The manifestation of the Spirit is given to each one for the profit of all" (1 Corinthians 12:7). This means that whatever gift you have, God didn't give it to you for *you*. He gave it so you could use it in some way for *someone else*. He blessed you with your spiritual gifts so you could be a blessing to those around you.

We have all been in situations where we needed help. I've had times when I needed to be exhorted and pushed a little bit toward truth. I've had times when I needed mercy. I've had times when I needed financial help. The wonderful truth about living within the body of Christ is that in those times, there were always people around me who had been specifically gifted to help me in those moments of need. That is a blessing!

Jesus said it this way: "For even the Son of Man did not come to be served, but to serve, and to give His life a ransom for many" (Mark 10:45). As we've noted throughout this study, Jesus is our ultimate example in all things. He is the prototype we are to emulate, just as He is the Lord we are to follow. Jesus said His mission on earth was not to be served, or be worshiped, or be made comfortable, but to *serve*. He used His gifts for the common good. Given this, how could our mission, purpose, or motivation for living be anything different?

3. When have you recently had an opportunity to serve others? What happened?

4. How do you typically feel when others make an effort to serve or bless you?

Spiritual Gifts Are
a Form of Stewardship

Someone might ask, "Why does God give us spiritual gifts in the first place?" Think about this. The Father is in heaven, Jesus is seated at His right hand, and the Holy Spirit dwells in you and me. How does God get His work done? The answer is through His people.

This means that using our spiritual gifts is not an option but a requirement. Specifically, the use of our spiritual gifts is a stewardship issue. As Peter put it, when we minister to others through our spiritual gifts, we are "good stewards." So when we fail to minister to others by using our spiritual gifts, we are *not* good stewards of what God has given to us.

On a practical level, let's say there is a group of impoverished children in a city close to where you live. You know from Scripture that it's God's desire for those children to be cared for—to have food, clothing, shelter, love, and compassion. So, how does God make that happen? The answer is that He has already positioned someone in that city who has the gift of mercy. When that person hears about those children, his or her heart is stirred to action.

God has also positioned someone in that city with the gift of giving and with the resources necessary to care for those children. And He has positioned someone else in that city with the gift of organization who can help pull everyone together and build a structure for connecting those who need help with those who want to help. This is how our gifts are supposed to operate—to minister to others and be a blessing to them.

Now, what if one or more of the people in this scenario refused to participate? What if they were unaware of their gifts or—even worse—refused to use those gifts in service to others? We would call this *bad stewardship*. God has called each of us to be good and faithful stewards of His resources. This includes your time, talents, treasures—and your spiritual gifts.

5. Do you consider yourself a "good steward" of the time, treasure, and talents God has given you? Why or why not? Explain.

....

....

....

....

....

....

....

6. What obstacles are hindering you from being a better steward of your spiritual gifts?

....

....

....

....

....

....

....

....

SPIRITUAL GIFTS BRING GLORY TO GOD

When I was attending seminary, I worked in a grocery store to help pay the bills. My primary job was to sweep the aisles and keep everything as clean as possible. One day, I heard the boss tell another employee, "Don't get in Stanley's way when he's working. He'll sweep you clean out of here!" I took pride in this. I worked fast and appreciated when others noticed my work. If I had a job that was nothing but sweeping, I was going to sweep with my best effort.

Later, I got a job in a textile mill. I really do believe it was close to Hades. It was so hot! I had to work way up high in the building . . . and you know how hot air rises. I only had to be there about thirty minutes before my shirt was soaked and my face was dripping with sweat. Still, I gave that job my best. I even prayed about it. "Lord, I don't like this very much, but I will stay here as long as You want me to. Please just help me stand the heat."

I share these stories because they illustrate the principle that Paul communicated in Colossians 3:23-24: "Whatever you do, do it heartily, as to the Lord and not to men, knowing that from the Lord you will receive the reward of the inheritance; for you serve the Lord Christ." You do your work *heartily*. Why? Because you are serving "as to the Lord and not to men." This certainly includes using your spiritual gifts.

People often believe that using their spiritual gifts will always be fun. Sadly, that is not true. Sometimes, being a good steward of your gifts means working hard. Actually, *most* times being a good steward of your gifts means working hard. It takes effort to serve others. It takes intentionality. It takes concentration, focus—and often a lot of time.

Perhaps this is why so many people quit. They start using their gifts and then discover the work is *hard*. Then they drop out of their ministry or stop volunteering. Or, worst of all, they try to squash and stem the voice of the Holy Spirit that stirs them and pushes them toward service. All simply because they do not want to do the hard work. This is a shame, because using your spiritual gifts is a wonderful way to serve others *and* glorify God. You show Him how much you value Him through obedience and hard work.

So remember this whenever you find yourself in a position to use your spiritual gifts: you are not working for your church, or for a ministry or a group of people in need, or even for yourself. Rather, you are working for Jesus. You have a chance right there, in that moment, to honor and glorify Him. So make it count!

7. What do you enjoy most about using your spiritual gifts? Why?

8. When has it felt like a burden to use your gifts to serve others?

WHY PEOPLE FAIL TO USE THEIR GIFTS

This leads us to a final question that I feel is worth addressing as we wrap up this lesson: *why do believers fail to serve God and weaken the testimony of the church by refusing to use their spiritual gifts?* I believe there are actually several reasons why this happens.

First, many people do not know Scripture. There are people—including followers of God—who have no earthly idea that God requires them to exercise their spiritual gifts and their talents. Thankfully, you are not among those people, because you have now learned quite a bit about what God expects throughout this study!

Second, many people are scared of making mistakes when they try to use their gifts. Perhaps they feel inadequate, or maybe they feel disqualified because of something in their past. They fall into the trap of evaluating themselves based on their own viewpoints—what they believe to be true about themselves. This is understandable, but it's not helpful. Instead, they need to evaluate themselves from God's viewpoint. They must make decisions based on what God *has declared* to be true about them. What God has declared is that they are *forgiven*. Not only that, but they are commanded to use their gifts. So there's no excuse.

Many people try to use their gifts, but they stop because the first or the second time didn't go as well as they had hoped. Maybe it even went badly. But this is how we *learn*. Just think about when you learned to swim. Did you just hop in the water and take off? No, you made mistakes and sank at times. But you tried again. This led to more mistakes and more sinking. But you kept trying—and failing—until you got the hang of it. Once you learned to swim, failure no longer had a pull on you, because you saw the progress you had made.

It's the same with your spiritual gifts. Don't give up on using them just because you have made mistakes. Don't give up even if you fail in some spectacular fashion. It is all part of learning—and you have a command to obey. So keep trying.

Finally, many people don't use their spiritual gifts to serve because they simply don't have the time. At least, this is what they claim. "I would like to help," they say, "but I just don't have the time." What this means is that they don't have time to *witness* to somebody else. They don't have time to *serve*. They don't have time to sing in the choir, or visit other people, or teach, or volunteer, even though they are gifted in these areas. They don't have any time to do anything for anybody . . . except, of course, for themselves.

I'll say this as plainly as I can: *this is pure selfishness*. It's ungodliness. And it is no excuse for disobeying God's command to minister to others through the use of our spiritual gifts.

God has called you to serve, and you need to obey. It is my desire that you would look at yourself today and say, "God, here I am. You know what I can do better than I do. I trust You to send me where I need to go. I know I have a spiritual gift. I have talents. And I have the Holy Spirit in me. So, God, I'm going to give it my best, beginning today. I'm listening for direction. I trust You, and I'm going to obey you. Help me to serve others so I can be a good steward of what You have given me. I want to bring glory to Your name in some small way."

9. Have you been using any of the excuses listed above?

10. What step can you take this week to serve others through your spiritual gift?

TODAY AND TOMORROW

Today: I am specifically called to use my spiritual gift to serve others.

Tomorrow: I will obey God's call to serve even when it is hard, and even when I don't feel like I have the time.

CLOSING PRAYER

Father, thank You for not making us all alike. You made us all wonderfully and excitingly different! Different temperaments. Different giftings. Thank You for these differences that exist in the body of Christ. Please use them to draw us closer together, so that we recognize the strengths in others that we need and do not possess. We are so grateful for Your love. Help us to never be satisfied with anything less than holy living—and wholly giving of ourselves to You—so that we might be used by You in every way possible.

Notes and Prayer Requests

Use this space to write any key points, questions, or prayer requests from this week's study.

THE GIFTS IN THE CHURCH

IN THIS LESSON

Learning: What are the benefits of using my spiritual gifts within the church?

Growing: How can I continue to be more effective and more committed as I serve the body of Christ?

Here's an assignment that may be easy or difficult depending on your season of life. Think back to a memorable Christmas season during your childhood. Do your best to picture where you were on that Christmas morning. The sights, smells, the sounds. The tension that built up between you and your siblings as you waited for your parents to allow you to open your gifts.

Now imagine opening one of your gifts. You hold the box in your hands and feel the smooth paper under your fingers. Maybe you were one of those kids who always shook the box a few times to get a sense of what might be in there. Or maybe you just tore into that paper as soon as it got near your fingers. Either way, the box is open. You reach inside, feel the gift, pull it out, and see . . . socks. A gift you didn't ask for and really do not want.

As a child, how did you respond? Even now as an adult, how do you respond when you receive a gift that doesn't really feel like a gift? Something you are not interested in receiving and do not have a way to use? I ask these questions because we need to address an issue that often comes up with the subject of spiritual gifts. Namely, some people value certain spiritual gifts above others. Some people believe that a few of the spiritual gifts listed in Scripture are more noble or more worthy of respect than others.

On a practical level, this can mean people are disappointed with the gift they receive from the Holy Spirit, just like a child receives a gift he or she doesn't really like on Christmas morning. Maybe, for example, you grew up in a family that valued the gift of exhortation. Maybe they overvalued it to the point where they expected it of you—and because you didn't receive it, you felt let down. For this reason, you now do not appreciate the gift you *did* receive from the Holy Spirit, because it wasn't the gift you believed to be most valuable.

This can also play out on the other side. Some people begin to feel pompous or arrogant about the spiritual gifts they did receive. Say, for instance, you have the gift of service, and you are keenly aware of the different ways you minister through that gift. You know exactly how much time, energy, and other resources you give so that you can serve. If you have an elevated view of your own gift, you might start to look down on those who have other gifts. *Mercy? That doesn't require any real effort. The gift of giving? All that means is having money and letting it go. The gift of service is clearly more valuable in the kingdom of God.*

Let me make it plain: there is no place in God's Word that gives followers of Christ the permission to project their gift or their beliefs about spiritual gifts onto others. None at all. None of us have the right to think of ourselves as less worthy—or to think of others as less worthy—because of the spiritual gifts that God has given to us.

The *Holy Spirit* is the one who distributes the spiritual gifts within the church. He is the one who determines that I have my gift, you have your gift, and everyone else has their gift. None of it is random. Rather, the Holy Spirit has distributed gifts throughout the church so that God's people can achieve the work that He has called them to do.

The key is *serving others in love* as the body of Christ. As we saw in the previous lesson, the purpose behind our gifts—the reason we have received them—is so we can serve and benefit others, starting within the church and then extending to the world. With that in mind, in this lesson we will look at how we are affected when we put our gifts into practice. Specifically, we gain four things when we use our gifts as the Holy Spirit intends: (1) greater confidence, (2) greater commitment, (3) greater effectiveness, and (4) greater joy.

1. Do you have a sense that some spiritual gifts are more admirable or worthwhile than others? Explain.

2. When have you encountered someone that looked down on or made light of your gifts and talents? How did you respond?

GREATER CONFIDENCE

First of all, once you have discovered your spiritual gift and understand the purpose behind it—once you know why you were gifted in the first place—you will have greater confidence when it comes to your role within the body of Christ. Many Christians today feel lost in the church. Even those who have been church members and church attenders all their lives can feel out of place. This is because they do not have a sense of how they fit. They do not have a sense of how they belong or how they can contribute to the work of the church.

When you first become part of a congregation, it is easy to get the sense that only what happens on stage on Sunday morning is important. You see the pastor up there preaching and teaching. You see the choir or a praise band up there singing. Everyone else is simply there to receive what has been offered. So, if you are not a preacher, or if you don't sing well or play an instrument, you can easily think, *I guess there's nothing for me to do here but sit and listen.*

This is why it is so critical for followers of Jesus to understand spiritual gifts. Once you learn the basic idea of gifts, you start to understand how you, as an individual, fit into the life of the church. You begin to think, *Okay, God, You have given me the gift of service—*

or *exhortation* or *mercy* or *teaching—and now I'm starting to understand these desires I've had to help others.*

Not only that, but once you understand how the gifts are supposed to operate within the church, you will become more confident when it comes to seeking out opportunities to use those gifts. When you know you have a responsibility to steward your gifts, you are no longer content to sit on the sideline. You want to find ways to get in the game!

3. When have you felt lost or out of place within the church?

4. How would you rate your level of confidence when it comes to actively using your spiritual gifts to serve within the church?

GREATER COMMITMENT

When you know your spiritual gifts and understand how to use them, you will also find a deeper sense of commitment in your service to the Lord. Confidence and commitment go hand in hand. The more confident you feel in your ability to serve—and serve effectively—the more committed you will become to maintaining a pattern of service.

Make no mistake—you were born to use your spiritual gift. As we have seen, it was given to you for a specific purpose. It is going to feel great for you when you start using your gift to match that purpose. It is going to feel *right*. Soon, you will want more. You will be ready to go deeper. You will find a greater sense of commitment to serving God and serving others.

Jesus said, "No one, having put his hand to the plow, and looking back, is fit for the kingdom of God" (Luke 9:62). Now, this is not a threat. Jesus is not seeking to put pressure on you or try to make you commit to something for which you are not ready. Rather, Jesus was highlighting the simple truth that you were designed to serve God. Paul states you were "created in Christ Jesus for good works, which God prepared beforehand" (Ephesians 2:10).

When you start to fulfill your destiny and put your hand to the work you were created to do, you are not going to look back. You are not going to turn aside. Rather, you will develop a greater commitment to obey Christ by serving Him and serving the church through your gifts.

5. When have you been surprised at your own effectiveness when using your spiritual gifts?

6. How would you rate your level of commitment when it comes to serving the church through your spiritual gifts? Explain.

....

....

....

....

....

....

....

GREATER EFFECTIVENESS

Next comes the issue of effectiveness. When you are ministering to others on the basis of your spiritual gifts, you will be more effective than when you try to minister based on your own talents or hard work. This is because your ministry will be empowered by the Holy Spirit, instead of you trying to rely completely on your own abilities.

In addition, the better you understand your giftedness, the better you will understand your strengths and weaknesses when it comes to using those gifts within the church. You will come to learn what works and what doesn't work. You will know when you are equipped and empowered by the Holy Spirit, rather than simply trying to will your way toward effectiveness.

The wonderful thing about spiritual gifts is how they make the church more effective as a whole. Your church community will benefit and become more effective at serving Christ when more and more of its members are aware of their spiritual gifts. Once again, as you and your fellow believers gain a better understanding of your strengths and weaknesses, you will find ways to work together. One person's strength will bolster the others' weakness, and vice versa.

When you are aware of your own spiritual gift *and* you gain a greater knowledge of the spiritual gifts of others, you soon start to have a way better understanding of why people respond to you the way they do. You become more effective at working with other members of your church. As an example, you might be someone who likes to make jokes. If you say something in a joking way to one person, he or she might laugh it off. But if you say the same thing to another person, he or she may feel like you struck them.

Why is this? Well, the second person might have the spiritual gift of mercy. That person feels things deeply. What seems like a joke to you really does hit him or her right between the eyes. The more you understand spiritual gifts, the more you understand the people who carry those gifts. And the more you understand people, the more you will understand why certain people act and react the way they do. You will find that you are more effective at managing those relationships in a way that is healthy and mutually beneficial.

This is especially true when it comes to friction within the church. Sometimes, you can have two people who are both genuinely trying to help and to serve within their congregations, but they have different ways of approaching things. They have different gifts, which means they have different values and different ways of seeking solutions and solving problems. When you don't understand those differences, you will encounter some heat. You'll find tension and even discouragement. But the more you understand that people can be both genuine in their service *and* different from you, the more effective you will be as a teammate in the body of Christ.

7. Where have you seen a lack of understanding cause tension or friction within the church?

8. How would you rate your effectiveness when it comes to using your spiritual gifts to serve God and others?

....

....

....

....

....

....

....

....

....

GREATER JOY

The final benefit you receive from using your spiritual gifts to serve the church is a greater experience of joy in your life. Let me tell you, that is a blessing you don't want to miss. There is nothing better than joy!

When you are doing what you are supposed to be doing, motivated by love and devotion to Christ, understanding the people around you, and pouring yourself out as an act of service both to them and with them . . . joy is the result. Joy is that inner sense of fulfillment and contentment that God gives you when you are functioning according to His plans for your life. In case you have not learned it already, God's designs and plans for you always include you using your spiritual gifts to serve.

There are plenty of people who drag themselves along in service to God. They minister to others the same way they wash dishes or take out the trash—just to get it done, because they know it needs to be done. This is not the way God designed the system to work. He gave you a unique and powerful set of gifts through the indwelling of His Holy Spirit. Even before the universe was formed, He made plans for you to use those gifts in a purposeful way. Whatever opportunities you have to use your spiritual gifts this week, God set those opportunities in motion *before He even created this world*. He has been planning and preparing for ages to give you the chance to use your spiritual gift to benefit others and bring glory to Himself.

When you step up and do what God has called you to do, you will feel joy. You will feel the incredible honor and wonder of living the way you were designed to live. Praise the Lord!

9. When have you felt great or been pleasantly surprised by an opportunity to serve others?

10. To what degree does using your spiritual gifts right now help you feel joy?

TODAY AND TOMORROW

Today: Understanding my spiritual gifts will allow me to better use those gifts within the church.

Tomorrow: I will strive for greater confidence, commitment, effectiveness, and joy as I use my spiritual gifts within the church.

CLOSING PRAYER

Father, we thank You and praise You and bless Your name for being so good to us. You love us enough to equip us to serve You and Your church. You have sealed us with the Holy Spirit. Baptized us into the body of Christ. And we know that You have given each of us a gift to use. Thank You that You didn't just save us and then leave us to struggle through life relying on just our human talents and abilities. You have granted us a spiritual gift for ministry. We bless Your name for blessing us and granting us this unique opportunity to serve You and Your family.

NOTES AND
PRAYER REQUESTS

Use this space to write any key points, questions, or prayer requests from this week's study.

Developing Your Motivational Gift

IN THIS LESSON

Learning: Now that I know my gift, what do I do with it?

Growing: Where can I use my gift?

Once you have identified your motivational ministry gift, you have a responsibility before God and to others to *develop* your gift. The ministry gift that you have been given by God is subject to your will for its operation. You must *choose* to use it. The Holy Spirit wants you to use your motivational gift at all times, and always for the benefit of the church.

As we have seen throughout this study, only Jesus Christ perfectly embodied all seven of the motivational gifts. He truly was the Prophet, Servant, Teacher, Exhorter, Giver, Leader, and Merciful One. The motivational gifts as a whole are a portrait of Jesus in action on earth and in our lives today through the ministry of the Holy Spirit.

Each of us has been given the privilege of displaying one facet of our Lord's ministry as a point of emphasis in our lives. It is as we work *together* bringing Christ to the world that we function as His *body*—the full manifestation of Christ that is capable of leading people to reconciliation with the Father, making disciples, and teaching by word and example.

1. "Give no offense . . . just as I also please all men in all things, not seeking my own profit, but the profit of many, that they may be saved. Imitate me, just as I also imitate Christ" (1 Corinthians 10:32–11:1). How did Jesus' life and ministry illustrate these verses? How did Paul imitate the example of Christ?

2. What did Paul mean when he said that he pleased all men in all things? How was this different from following the teachings of the world?

MOVING BEYOND YOUR OWN MINISTRY GIFT

Faithfulness to our own motivational gift does not mean that we cannot step into other ministry roles. For example, assume that your church needs people to direct the parking so the lot is orderly and the church services can begin promptly. Helping to park cars is a ministry that is often undertaken joyfully and successfully by those who have the motivational gift of service.

But let's say your particular gift is exhortation. Helping with the parking lot is not a ministry to which you would naturally gravitate, or in which you would find satisfaction week after week. But on any given Sunday, should there be a lack of people to help with this ministry, you certainly would be capable of assisting in it.

The Holy Spirit will help you to function outside of your motivational gift *if the need arises*. On the whole, however, you are going to find the greatest satisfaction, fulfillment, and success when you operate within your motivational gift. It would be both presumptuous and prideful to say to another person, "Oh, I can't help you with that urgent need right now—that isn't my ministry gift." When crises arise, the Holy Spirit's grace can help any believer to respond effectively, as long as that believer is willing to be used and empowered by the Spirit.

However, let's say you are gifted as a teacher. It would be wise of you to say, "Oh, yes, I can teach Sunday school this year," but unwise for you to say, "Oh, yes, I will take on the responsibilities of organizing the ministry to those who are homebound or in nursing homes." If you are gifted in teaching, you will find fulfillment as a teacher. You may be *capable* of leading the nursing-home ministry, but you will not find that work as fulfilling nor be as effective at it.

Using this same example, recognize that it would be an act of disobedience to the Lord for a person gifted as a teacher to decline a teaching opportunity out of rebellion, false humility, or misplaced priorities. God has given you a gift for you to *use*, and He will always present ample opportunities for you to do so. So be open to the ways in which the Holy Spirit may lead you into opportunities to use your gifts—even though you may be a bit fearful or concerned about how well you may do in the ministry role presented to you. This is a natural response, even if you are gifted in a particular area. Say *yes* to the Lord, and then trust the Holy Spirit to help you use your gift to the best of your ability.

3. "All things are lawful for me, but not all things are helpful; all things lawful for me, but not all things edify. Let no one seek his own, but each one the other's well-being" (1 Corinthians 10:23-24). What is the main purpose of the motivational gifts? How can a person know when they are being used correctly?

....

....

....

....

....

....

....

4. How might these verses apply in situations of special needs, such as the parking lot illustration given above?

....

....

....

....

....

....

....

Manifesting the Fruit and Gifts of the Spirit

As believers within the church, the body of Christ, we are to manifest the ministry of Jesus Christ to the world. Part of this means that we are to bear the likeness of the Holy Spirit into the world. The fruit of the Spirit is demonstrated in our positive character as we employ our gifts. Furthermore, we should be willing at all times to demonstrate any and all of the gifts of the Holy Spirit should He desire to use us for His ministry purposes.

We are to be clean and pure vessels through which the Holy Spirit might pour His power, love, wisdom, and assistance. The spiritual gifts, which are often called the "gifts of the Spirit" (such as those identified in 1 Corinthians 12:8-10), belong to the Holy Spirit and are given by the Holy Spirit. They are aspects of the Holy Spirit's own power that He imparts to believers so they might minister more effectively to others. In the operation of these spiritual gifts, it is the Holy Spirit who provides the motivation to believers to act in specific ways at specific times and for specific purposes. As believers are obedient to the Holy Spirit and allow His work within them, they acts *as Jesus would act* in meeting the need in another person's life.

These spiritual gifts are not innate in the believer. They reside in the Holy Spirit. They are not for the benefit of the believer through whom they function. They are for the benefit of another person who is experiencing need or trouble. The person working out of his or her giftedness should not seek his or her own glory. All praise and honor should be given to God as the giver of gifts, who empowers us to serve in His name and for His purposes.

The difference between these spiritual gifts and the motivational gifts is that the spiritual gifts Paul lists in 1 Corinthians 12:8-10 reside in the Holy Spirit and operate totally at His will. The motivational gifts reside in us. They are imparted to us on a *permanent basis* by the Holy Spirit at the time of our acceptance of Jesus Christ as Savior, and they are never removed from our lives. They operate to a great extent as we will them to operate . . . in other words, as we develop them and choose to use them.

5. "To one is given the word of wisdom through the Spirit, to another the word of knowledge through the same Spirit, to another faith by the same Spirit, to another gifts of healings by the same Spirit" (1 Corinthians 12:8–9). What is significant about Paul's repeated use of "through the same Spirit" in this passage?

6. When have you seen a "gift of the Spirit" at work in your life?

DEVELOPING YOUR SPIRITUAL GIFTS

The development of your spiritual gift begins with an act of faith in the Lord Jesus Christ that He can and will work through you. You must be obedient first to what you know is true about God the Father, Jesus Christ, and the work of the Holy Spirit. Again, as James wrote, "Be doers of the word, and not hearers only" (James 1:22).

You are prepared and made ready for service as you turn from sin and disobedience, choose to believe in Jesus Christ, trust God in all things, and obey God's commandments and the leading of the Holy Spirit. The Holy Spirit indwells us as believers, and He will prepare us and empower us for ministry. At that point, as we discussed in the last lesson, your faith and obedience will *compel* you to use your gift—you will find that you cannot *not* act.

God has called you to develop your ministry gift in four specific ways. *First, walk in the Holy Spirit daily.* Repent of any willful pride in choosing to do things your way and intentionally yield control of your life to the Holy Spirit. Give God permission to work in you and through you. Ask for the help and guidance of the Holy Spirit on a daily basis, and be sensitive at all times to the opportunities the Holy Spirit is placing in your path.

Second, learn all you can about the characteristics of your particular ministry gift. Your prayer should continually be, "Lord, help me to understand this precious gift that You have given to me and to know how best to develop it and use it." The best source for learning about your particular motivational gift is the Word of God. Read everything that Jesus had to say about your gift. Read what Paul, John, and others in the New Testament wrote about the employment of your gift. Grow in your understanding of how God wants you to use your gift.

Third, focus on the development of your gift. Concentrate on the gift you have been given. Run the race the Lord has put before you—and run with diligence, focus, and patience (see Hebrews 12:1). Run with a single-minded goal of becoming an expert contributor of your gift to the body of Christ, with your eyes continually on the Lord and on His desires (see 1 Corinthians 9:24). Put aside any distractions and refuse to take any detours. Readjust your priorities so that your number-one emphasis is on the godly use of your ministry gift in as many situations as possible—at home, on the job, in the community, and especially in your church.

Fourth, get involved in a ministry and use your gift to the best of your ability. Motivational gifts are developed through use. Find a ministry about which you care deeply and offer your services (your gift). Get involved. The more you use your gift, the stronger you will become in it, the more effective you will be, and the greater benefit you will render to the body of Christ. Paul wrote that we are to be like athletes in training when it comes to the exercise of our ministry gift. A good training program requires regular and consistent effort. So, too, the employment of your motivational gifts. You must get involved and stay involved.

7. "Do you not know that those who run in a race all run, but one receives the prize? Run in such a way that you may obtain it. And everyone who competes for the prize is temperate in all things. Now they do it to obtain a perishable crown, but we for an imperishable crown" (1 Corinthians 9:24–25). How does an athlete "run in such a way" that he or she obtains the first prize? What is involved?

8. "In a great house there are not only vessels of gold and silver, but also of wood and clay, some for honor and some for dishonor. Therefore if anyone cleanses himself from the latter, he will be a vessel for honor, sanctified and useful for the Master, prepared for every good work" (2 Timothy 2:20–21). What is a "vessel for honor"? How is it different from a vessel used for dishonorable purposes? What is required of a Christian if he or she is to be "fit" for the use of the Holy Spirit?

CALLED TO BEAR FRUIT

Jesus called His disciples to bear fruit—in fact, He told them to bear "much fruit" (John 15:8). It is in your fruitfulness that Jesus Christ is expressed to the world and the Father is glorified. You will become fruitful as you trust God to work in your life and learn to walk day by day in the Spirit, learning all that you can about your ministry gift, focusing on its development, and using it at every opportunity. In fact, you cannot *help* but be fruitful, because it is the Holy Spirit who will be producing fruit in you and through you.

As Jesus taught, "Abide in Me, and I in you. As the branch cannot bear fruit of itself, unless it abides in the vine, neither can you, unless you abide in Me. I am the vine, you are the branches. He who abides in Me, and I in him, bears much fruit; for without Me you can do nothing" (John 15:4–5). Choose to abide in the Lord and be obedient to His call on your life. Be true to the motivational ministry gift that He has given you.

9. What does it mean to *abide* in Christ? Why is this abiding necessary when using motivational gifts? What happens when you try to use your gifts apart from Christ?

10. "I say then: Walk in the Spirit, and you shall not fulfill the lust of the flesh" (Galatians 5:16). What does it mean to "walk in the Spirit"? How is this done on a daily basis?

TODAY AND TOMORROW

Today: God has given me a gift that is vital
to the health of His body.

Tomorrow: I will ask Him this week to teach me
how to use my gift to His glory.

CLOSING PRAYER

Father, we thank You for the beautiful example of Jesus. He never served You for Himself. He served You out of love. Would You examine our hearts, sift our motivations, and help us to face ourselves as we really are—not as we want to be or as we think other people see us, but just as we really are? We want to labor for You out of love and devotion for Your grace and goodness. And today, we pray that those of us who have not yet identified our motivational gift will make a commitment to continue seeking to discover it. We want to use everything that You have provided to minister to others in obedience to You. Let us come to know our gift, to develop it, and then exercise it in love. In this way, we know that we will be following the example of Christ.

NOTES AND PRAYER REQUESTS

Use this space to write any key points, questions, or prayer requests from this week's study.

LEADER'S GUIDE

Thank you for choosing to lead your group through this Bible study from Dr. Charles F. Stanley on *Ministering Through Spiritual Gifts*. The rewards of being a leader are different from those of participating, and it is our prayer that your own walk with Jesus will be deepened by this experience. During the twelve lessons in this study, you will be helping your group members explore and discuss key themes about how they can discover and use the particular motivational gifts that God has instilled in them from the moment of their birth. There are multiple components in this section that can help you structure your lessons and discussion time, so please be sure to read and consider each one.

BEFORE YOU BEGIN

Before your first meeting, make sure your group members each have a copy of *Ministering Through Spiritual Gifts* so they can follow along in the study guide and have their answers written out ahead of time. Alternately, you can hand out the study guides at your first meeting and give the group members some time to look over the material and ask any preliminary questions. During your first meeting, be sure to send a sheet around the room and have the members write down their name, phone number, and email address so you can keep in touch with them during the week.

To ensure everyone has a chance to participate in the discussion, the ideal size for a group is around eight to ten people. If there are more than ten people, break up the bigger group into smaller subgroups. Make sure the members are committed to participating each week, as this will help create stability and help you better prepare the structure of the meeting.

At the beginning of each meeting, you may wish to start the group time by asking the group members to provide their initial reactions to the material they have read during the week. The goal is to just get the group members' preliminary thoughts—so encourage them at this point to keep their answers brief. Ideally, you want everyone in the group to get a chance to share some of their thoughts, so try to keep the responses to a minute or less.

Give the group members a chance to answer, but tell them to feel free to pass if they wish. With the rest of the study, it's generally not a good idea to have everyone answer every question—a free-flowing discussion is more desirable. But with the opening icebreaker questions, you can go around the circle. Encourage shy people to share, but don't force them. Also, try to keep any one person from dominating the discussion so everyone will have the opportunity to participate.

WEEKLY PREPARATION

As the group leader, there are a few things you can do to prepare for each meeting:

- *Be thoroughly familiar with the material in the lesson.* Make sure you understand the content of each lesson so you know how to structure the group time and are prepared to lead the group discussion.

- *Decide, ahead of time, which questions you want to discuss.* Depending on how much time you have each week, you may not be able to reflect on every question. Select specific questions that you feel will evoke the best discussion.

- *Take prayer requests.* At the end of your discussion, take prayer requests from your group members and then pray for one another.

- *Pray for your group.* Pray for your group members throughout the week and ask God to lead them as they study His Word.

- *Bring extra supplies to your meeting.* The members should bring their own pens for writing notes, but it's a good idea to have extras available for those who forget. You may also want to bring paper and additional Bibles.

STRUCTURING THE GROUP DISCUSSION TIME

You will need to determine with your group how long you want to meet each week so you can plan your time accordingly. Generally, most groups like to meet for either sixty minutes or ninety minutes, so you could use one of the following schedules:

SECTION	60 Minutes	90 Minutes
WELCOME (group members arrive and get settled)	5 minutes	10 minutes
ICEBREAKER (group members share their initial thoughts regarding the content in the lesson)	10 minutes	15 minutes
DISCUSSION (discuss the Bible study questions you selected ahead of time)	35 minutes	50 minutes
PRAYER/CLOSING (pray together as a group and dismiss)	10 minutes	15 minutes

As the group leader, it is up to you to keep track of the time and keep things moving according to your schedule. If your group is having a good discussion, don't feel the need to stop and move on to the next question. Remember, the purpose is to pull together ideas and share unique insights on the lesson. Encourage everyone to participate, but don't be concerned if certain group members are more quiet. They may just be internally reflecting on the questions and need time to process their ideas before they can share them.

GROUP DYNAMICS

Leading a group study can be a rewarding experience for you and your group members—but that doesn't mean there won't be challenges. Certain members may feel uncomfortable in discussing topics that they consider very personal and might be afraid of being called on. Some members might have disagreements on specific issues. To help prevent these scenarios, consider establishing the following ground rules:

- If someone has a question that may seem off topic, suggest that it is discussed at another time, or ask the group if they are okay with addressing that topic.

- If someone asks a question to which you do not know the answer, confess that you don't know and move on. If you feel comfortable, you can invite the other group members to give their opinions or share their comments based on personal experience.

- If you feel like a couple of people are talking much more than others, direct questions to people who may not have shared yet. You could even ask the more dominating members to help draw out the quiet ones.

- When there is a disagreement, encourage the members to process the matter in love. Invite members from opposing sides to evaluate their opinions and consider the ideas of the other members. Lead the group through Scripture that addresses the topic, and look for common ground.

When issues arise, encourage your group to follow these words from Scripture: "Love one another" (John 13:34), "If it is possible, as much as depends on you, live peaceably with all men" (Romans 12:18), "Whatever things are true . . . noble . . . pure . . . lovely . . . if there is any virtue and if there is anything praiseworthy—meditate on these things" (Philippians 4:8), and "Be swift to hear, slow to speak, slow to wrath" (James 1:19). This will make your group time more rewarding and beneficial for everyone who attends.

Thank you again for your willingness to lead your group. May God reward your efforts and dedication, equip you to guide your group in the weeks ahead, and make your time together in *Ministering Through Spiritual Gifts* fruitful for His kingdom.

Also Available from Charles F. Stanley

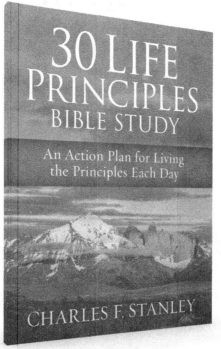

9780310082521 Softcover

30 LIFE PRINCIPLES BIBLE STUDY
An Action Plan for Living the Principles Each Day

During his many years of ministry, Dr. Charles Stanley has faithfully highlighted the 30 life principles that have guided him and helped him to grow in his knowledge, service, and love of God. In this Bible study, you will explore each of these principles in depth and learn how to make them a part of your everyday life. As you do, you will find yourself growing in your relationship with Christ and on the road to the future God has planned for you.

Available now at your favorite bookstore.

THOMAS NELSON
Since 1798

Also Available in the
CHARLES F. STANLEY
Bible Study Series

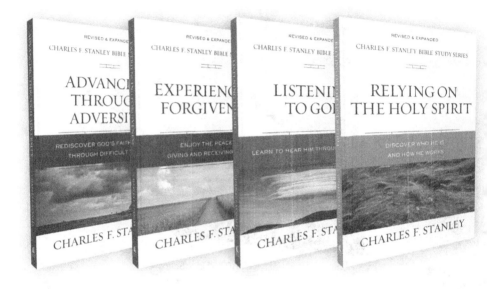

Each study draws on Dr. Stanley's many years of teaching the guiding principles found in God's Word, showing how we can apply them in practical ways to every situation we face. This edition of the series has been completely revised and updated, and includes two brand-new lessons from Dr. Stanley.

Available now at your favorite bookstore.
More volumes coming soon.

The Charles F. Stanley Bible Study Series is a unique
approach to Bible study, incorporating biblical truth,
personal insights, emotional responses,
and a call to action.

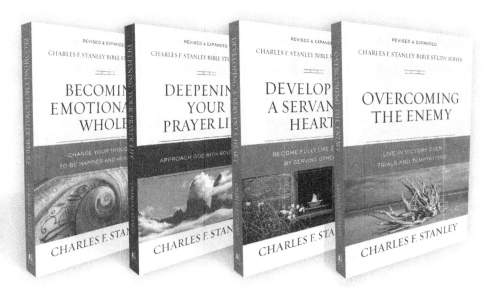

9780310106555	Advancing Through Adversity	9780310105626	Developing a Servant's Heart
9780310106579	Experiencing Forgiveness	9780310105602	Overcoming the Enemy
9780310106593	Listening to God	9780310105640	Developing Inner Strength
9780310106616	Relying on the Holy Spirit	9780310105664	Ministering Through Spiritual Gifts
9780310105565	Becoming Emotionally Whole	9780310105688	Discovering Your Identity
9780310105589	Deepening Your Prayer Life	9780310105701	Practicing Basic Spiritual Disciplines

THOMAS NELSON
Since 1798